The Miracle
The Kent
of

W.E.   Loss of the Halswell East Indiaman, Capt. Pierce.

The Miracle of The Kent

A TALE
of
COURAGE,
FAITH,
and
FIRE

NICHOLAS TRACY

WESTHOLME
Yardley

Frontispiece: *The Loss of the Halswell, East Indiaman, Capt Pierce* by E.W., published by Thomas Tegg. See page 66. (*NMM PAD6346*)

First Westholme Paperback March 2014

Westholme Publishing, LLC
904 Edgewood Road
Yardley, Pennsylvania 19067
Visit our Web site at www.westholmepublishing.com

ISBN: 978-1-59416-202-2
Also available as an eBook

Printed in the United States of America on acid-free paper.

They that go down to the sea in ships, that do business in great waters; these see the works of the Lord, and his wonders in the deep. For he commandeth, and raiseth the stormy wind, which lifteth up the waves thereof. They mount up to the heaven, they go down again to the depths: their soul is melted because of trouble. They reel to and fro, and stagger like a drunken man, and are at their wit's end. Then they cry unto the Lord in their trouble, and he bringeth them out of their distresses.

—*Psalm 107: 23–28*

Then was there tumult. The sea was stirred. The horn-fish played, gliding through the deep, and above circled the grey sea-mew, greedy of prey. The sun grew dark and the winds arose. Waves broke and seas ran high. The rigging moaned. Billows swept them, and water-terror grew in the welter of waves.

—*from the Andreas, Anon. ca. 900–1000*

One cannot help concluding that he who sees nothing of a Divine Providence in our preservation must be lamentably and willfully blind to the majesty of the Lord.

—*Major Duncan MacGregor,* Kent *survivor*

Contents

The Burning of the Kent (1825) by Jean Antoine Théodore Gudin. (*Musée de la Marine, Paris*)

Preface

A Letter to a Friend

My Dear E,

With the twofold view of gratifying the lively interest excited in the minds of our friends, by the awful and afflicting calamity that has lately befallen the Kent East Indiaman, and of humbly recording the signal interposition of that God "who, in the midst of judgment, remembereth mercy," I am induced to transmit to you—to be disposed of as you may think fit—the following detailed account of the melancholy event, which has at once deprived the country of many valuable lives, and thereby plunged numerous families into the deepest distress, and involved, I fear, in pecuniary ruin, or reduced to extreme embarrassment, most of the gallant survivors.

So begins a "Letter to a Friend by a Passenger." It was published soon after the survivors came ashore as a *Narrative of the Loss of the Kent East Indiaman, by fire, in the Bay of Biscay, on March 1,*

1825, and it is now known that the passenger and author was Major Duncan MacGregor, later General Sir Duncan MacGregor. He had been onboard the *Kent* until shortly before she blew up, and, as he wrote, never thought to survive the night. Who "E" was remains unknown. MacGregor's account was an instant success. Susan Darwin recommended it to her naturalist brother Charles as "very interesting . . . I advise you to read it if you can meet with it."[1] Forty-one years later, Charles Dickens remarked that "It is sometimes difficult to understand why certain events rouse a whole country. . . . The loss of the *Kent* East Indiaman is remembered, and discussed with an interest that shows that sympathy in the event is still existing." He attributed it to the "peculiar heroism or pathos" of the event "which touches the national heart."[2]

As a soldier and as an evangelist, MacGregor was deeply interested in the manner in which the victims met their fate, with courage and faith, or with drunkenness and disaster. His terrific story of the loss of the *Kent* by fire and storm was to become one of the staples of nineteenth-century literature; it was reprinted repeatedly throughout the century and again in the 1970s. The narrative shows some of the characteristics of a work cleaned up for public readership, but it is not the only account we have of the disaster, nor even the only one by MacGregor. A letter he wrote to his father soon after being brought safely ashore was published by Edwin Hodder in 1894 at the beginning of his biography of John "Rob Roy" MacGregor, Duncan's son who survived the disaster as a newborn baby. This account is far more immediate and personal. Duncan MacGregor was a great man who inspired everyone around him, and this is evident in both the published narrative and in his letter to his father.[3]

Official reports of the disaster were written to the Commander-in-Chief of the Army, the Duke of York, by Lieutenant Colonel

Robert Bryce Fearon commanding the right wing of the 31st Regiment taking passage on the *Kent*, and to the Court of Directors of the East India Company by the *Kent*'s captain, Henry Cobb. There must have been many private letters from survivors, but apart from Major MacGregor's to his father, the only others that are known to have survived, at least in transcription, are three letters written by Dr. Edward Richard Townsend who was onboard in the capacity of Assistant Surgeon in the company's service, and one by Captain Edward William Bray who was third in command of the 31st Regiment. Townsend had been intent on making his fortune in India, but his hopes were so shattered by the disaster that he returned quietly to his native Cork, in Ireland, and spent the rest of his life there. His first letter is a brief note to his sister Mary who lived on Queen's Street, Cork; a fuller account to her a few days later was also addressed to his mother and to his brother, the Reverend Edward Townsend in Ballincollig, and a third which is almost a copy of the latter, to his sister Mary.[4] Captain Bray's letter was written to Loftus A. Bryan in Dublin.[5]

One of the obituaries published following Dr. Townsend's death in 1878, credits Townsend with being the author of a second narrative of the end of the *Kent*. This reference can only be to the short pamphlet printed in Falmouth, Cornwall, two weeks after the survivors were brought ashore there by the *Cambria*, nearly naked and exhausted, having lost all their property, and mourning their loved ones who had drowned. But the attribution to Townsend is probably wrong. Boase and Courtney's *Bibliotheca Cornubiensis* published in 1878 credits the second narrative to a Reverend Edgcombe Rimmell who was the son of a Falmouth man. Reverend Rimmell almost certainly grew up there and in 1825 would have been 22 years old. Six years later he was appointed Curate of Mabe near

Falmouth. Nevertheless, there are similarities in the content of Townsend's letters and the second narrative to suggest that he may have provided much of the detail even if he were not the author.[6]

The voices of the common soldiers and seamen can be heard in the testimony taken by Colonel Fearon for the War Department and by journalists who interviewed the survivors. The sensational nature of the story ensured that the *Times* of London, the *Royal Cornwall Gazette*, and the *West Briton and Cornwall Advertiser* printed extensive reports.

Several seaman artists undertook pictures of the subject, providing a seamen's perspective to complement MacGregor's soldierly one. The most dramatic picture was by Thomas Buttersworth, who painted the subject after dark, with the light from the fire amidships glaring though the stern windows, and illuminating boats from the *Cambria* battling the wild sea to get the people off.[7] The pictures engraved by William Daniell show more detail of the ship hove to in a heavy sea, on fire, and showing men letting themselves down a rope from the spanker boom into boats, the crews of which were trying to steady them underneath to receive the survivors.

Like the majority of painters who worked with marine subjects, Buttersworth was himself a sailor, and his patrons expected a high degree of representational accuracy.[8] It is to be supposed he talked with the officers of the *Kent*, and possibly those of the brigs *Cambria* and *Caroline* that rescued her people, before he set to work painting his picture of the subject. Although William Daniell was not himself a professional seaman, he had such experience of East India Company shipping as a young man that he may almost be considered in that light.[9] In 1810, Daniell and his Uncle Thomas published a volume of plates from drawings made during their voyages on Indiamen, entitled *A Picturesque Voyage to India by the Way of China*.[10] In 1823, William Daniell returned to the subject.

The reviewer in the *Literary Gazette* was so impressed he wrote that "Mr. Daniell's engraving of 'An Indiaman in a North-Wester,' and 'Man Overboard, off the Cape,' have made every lover of the Fine Arts acquainted with his tremendous powers and appalling fidelity in subjects of this description."[10] Daniell painted his picture of the *Kent, East Indiaman on Fire in the Bay of Biscay* in 1825 "from authentic information," and in 1826, he exhibited a companion picture of the survivors being taken by boat to the brig *Cambria*.[12] A Francis Daniell was second mate of the *Kent* on its second voyage, in 1824, and it is possible he had some family connection with the artist.[13]

The work begun by Buttersworth and Daniell was followed by other artists who found there was a continuing interest in pictures of the subject. Thomas Marie Madawaska Hemy (1851–1937) painted a picture of the rescue, which was named *Just in Time* when it was published in the January 27, 1894, issue of *The Boy's Own Paper*. It was published again in the 1911 issue of Joseph Bibby's *Annual*, and was hand painted about the same time on a glass lantern slide for distribution by the Church Army.[14]

The narratives were repeatedly abstracted in nineteenth-century papers and anthologies, and a fictionalized version of the events appeared in 1865 when William Russell published a collection of sea stories called *The Jolly Boat* that included a supposed account by one James Bolton, who described himself as a "cadet, rising sixteen, in the service of the Honourable East-India Company." On the beach before departure our hero met and fell for Fanny Barton, "a singularly charming child, joyous as a bird," who was traveling with her mother to India.[15]

The story of the *Kent* disaster and rescue caught the attention of the public because it was an era in which thousands of people were on the move around the world seeking new and better lives. The

soldier passengers on the *Kent* were going to India, and onboard
the ship that led the rescue, the *Cambria*, were Cornish miners seeking their fortunes in Mexico. The dangers of the sea were very much
on people's minds, as was the sorrow of departure. But there was
more to it than the immediate concerns of travelers. When eight
years later James Hedderwick put the story of the *Kent* into an
anthology which he called *The English Orator*, he commented:
"there is a something in the misfortunes which happen at sea, that
awakens in our bosoms a more than ordinary sympathy with the
sufferers. The loneliness of the ocean is, even in idea, fearful to the
mind, and the complete separation of those who are on its paths
from the rest of mankind makes us follow them in our sympathies,
as if they had once been sharers of our home."[16] The events held
the public interest for so many years because their principal narra-
tor, Duncan MacGregor, had caught their deep psychological
importance.

In life's voyage, ships, fires at sea, storm, and heroic rescues are
metaphors of the intense activity required for survival, punctuated
by the long hours of stoic endurance during which the emotions of
fear and hope alternate in a macabre dance. The story of the *Kent*
was important not only for what happened onboard the ships and
in the boats, but also for what did not happen.

The *Kent* was only one of many ships to be destroyed at sea. The
best known story of maritime disaster was the loss of the *Titanic* in
1912. But the story of the *Kent* stands in contrast with the worst
tragedies of the era because of the redeeming qualities of the people
involved, not only MacGregor himself, but the captains of the three
ships, Henry Cobb, William Cook, and Robert Bibby; and the passengers themselves, the soldiers with battle honors from the
Napoleonic war, and the world's most respected hard-rock miners.
All of them worked together to ensure maximum survival in condi-

tions where great loss would have been thought to be inevitable—
a striking cooperation that ensured the greatest number of lives
saved under the most deadly conditions.

The East Indiaman *Repulse* (1820) in the East India Dock Basin by Charles Henry Seaforth. (*NMM PY0536*)

I

Fitting Out

THIS IS A STORY OF THREE SHIPS, their commanders, the ship's companies, and their passengers, most of whom were soldiers of the 31st Regiment of Foot and their families, employees of the Honorable East India Company, and Cornish miners and Yorkshire smelterers. It was the tides of empire and of commerce that were to bring together these three ships in an empty quarter of the Bay of Biscay on a day of storm and fire.

By 1825, the East India Company, which was then over two hundred years old, had all but become an instrument of the British government. The process of bringing the company under complete government control would be completed in 1833 when it was stripped entirely of its commercial rights. When it had first been incorporated in 1600 by Royal Charter, it was no more than a trading company, accorded monopoly control of English commerce with India to enable it to support an establishment that included fortified storehouses. But in the following century and a half it had acquired the status of a political power through the expansion of its relationship with the Mogul rulers.

In 1756 the savage action of the Nawab of Bengal's soldiers that led to the deaths of many Britons in the notorious Black Hole of Calcutta caused a reaction as tremendous in its extent as did the attack on the World Trade Center in New York on September 11, 2001. Although it had continued to protest that it was only interested in trade, the company had gone on the offensive, reducing the Moguls to puppet rulers. This transformation was recognized in 1773 when the British parliament passed the East India Company Act appointing the company governor of Bengal, Warren Hastings, the Governor General of British India, and establishing a British judiciary. But there was concern in England about the political implications of the huge wealth being acquired by the company through its territorial control. Eleven years later William Pitt strengthened British control over the political power of the company by creating a Board of Commissioners for the Affairs of India, or Board of Control, presided over by a secretary of state, and attended by the Chancellor of the Exchequer and by four privy councillors nominated by the king. In 1786, the political power of the governor general was further strengthened by permitting the office to be held by the commander-in-chief of British forces in India.

The division of the commercial and political roles of the company, and the threat posed by Napoleon's 1798 Egyptian campaign, which was intended as a step to a French invasion of India, stimulated a vigorous expansion of British power in India. The company came to control all of India, except for the Punjab, Sind, and Nepal. Indian princes were reduced to the status of vassals of the company.

In keeping with its growing imperial role, company headquarters at East India House in Leadenhall Street, London, had been decorated in 1778 with a ceiling painting by the Italian artist Spiridione Roma, who named his work *The East Offering Its Riches to Britannia*. Around this masterpiece the building was rebuilt by Richard Jupp, the company surveyor, between 1799 and 1800 in a neo-Paladian style.

The problem of transforming traditional Indian society into a nineteenth-century economy was taken seriously by the company. To prepare "writers"—the company bureaucrats—for their work in India, in 1805 the company opened a school near the manor of Hailey, in Hertfordshire. The following year it commissioned William E. Wilkins, who later designed the National Gallery, to draw a neo-classical design for Haileybury College around a large grass quadrangle. The influential economist Thomas Robert Malthus was employed there as professor of history and political economy from 1805 until his death in 1834. David Ricardo was another economist whose ideas were accepted by the company, which applied his rent theory in India. The liberal philosophers and politicians James and John Stuart Mill were both employed by the company and active in framing legislation for India, and in doing so, were influenced by the theory of utility propounded by Jeremy Bentham.

As the effective government of most of India, the company governor-general and commander-in-chief had responsibility for its defense. The company had developed its own Indian army, but it also needed the close cooperation of the Royal Army and the Royal Navy, although it was not above trying to do their friends out of their accustomed prize money. The company's ships had an important role in the transport of British regiments and company officers to and from postings in India. On the *Kent's* second voyage, in

1822–23, she had as passengers part of the 13th Light Infantry. One of the children of the regiment was Sarah Speedy, then aged seven, traveling with two sisters to India. In her memoirs she recalled only her "Grandma Eastfield hooking my pelisse. It was purple, trimmed with swans down, and the dear old lady kissed me while she knelt to hook it for me when we were leaving her to go on board." Life for people of the British Raj was made up of such departures, often never to return. Sarah also recalled the time a shark was hooked, and when hauled on board how it banged an old woman on the head with its tail, knocking her out cold.[1]

THE *Kent* was one of the great ships of the Honorable East India Company and was commanded by Captain Henry Cobb, one of the most experienced in their service. Born in England, Cobb first went to sea in their ships in 1802 as a midshipman, or "guinea pig," in the *Europe*, 202 years after the formation of the original company. When built in 1820, the *Kent* was specifically intended for Cobb's command.[2] She was employed in the triangular trade between London and Bombay or Bengal in India, and homeward by way of Canton in China.

The East India Company did not own its ships. For nearly two centuries the ships employed by the company had been built by an exclusive coterie of proprietors, but in 1796 the Court of Directors confirmed bylaws providing for secret tenders for the freight and demurrage of six voyages, specifying the burthen, dimensions, and the sizes of scantlings, timber, and planks to which the ship should conform. This had been confirmed by act of Parliament in July 1799.[3] Quite literally, demurrage means the cost to the owner of having a ship tied to the harbor wall. The main concern was to reduce the incentive for commanders to divert from their passage in order to undertake private trade. The lowest tenderer was invited to provide a new ship, which he then built in a private yard. The requirement that tenders were always to be made for at least six voyages was intended to minimize the bids by guaranteeing that the capital costs would not have to be covered in the first voyage. In the nineteenth century, the number of voyages a ship was permitted to make increased to eight and even more, reflecting the greater life expectancy of ships built of teak at Bombay.

Stewart Marjoribanks, who was a director of the company, had been awarded the contract and had ordered the *Kent* built at Wigram and Green's yard at Blackwall on the Thames. She was the seventh ship with that name to serve the company. When she was measured by the customs surveyor "on the ground" on November 23, 1820, and then registered, she was found to have been given an extreme length "aloft" of 169 feet, 2 inches, with a beam of 43 feet, 3 inches, and a tonnage of 1,421 91/94 ths (thousands).* She was described as a square-stemmed ship with poop and forecastle decks, and quarter galleries. She was "frigate built," with a single row of gun ports, fully decked amidships, and without the extreme tumble-home of earlier Indiamen. As a ship-rigged vessel she had three masts, and she was built with three decks.

Two days after the custom's survey, Marjoribanks, who resided at the King's Arms Yard near the Guildhall, sold a share in her to a neighbor of his, one William Kershaw. By act of Parliament, the

---

*The tonnage value was derived from the "Builders old Measurement Formula" which was used to determine how much cargo could be carried in the hold: Tonnage = (Length – 3/5 Beam) x Beam x 2 Beam / 94. Just how inexact was the system is shown by the fact that, when in the new year *Kent* was remeasured by the survey officer for the Board of Trade Registrar of Shipping after she was launched, he recorded her tonnage as only 1,365 25/94 ths.[4]

ownership of all ships was divided into 64 shares; Kershaw purchased two of them, or 1/32 share.[5] The *Kent* was launched on
December 16, 1820, and in the new year, as she fitted out,
Marjoribanks continued to diversify the ownership. It was customary for commanders in East India Company service to own a share
in the ship in order to encourage them to seek a profitable voyage.
On February 16, 1821, Marjoribanks accordingly sold a 1/16 share
to Henry Cobb, which was shown on the Board of Trade register as
1/15th of Marjoribank's interest or "right" in the ship. Four days
later he sold three 1/16th shares to George Reed and William
Thomson of Wapping Wall, to William Cotton of Crosby Square,
and to Charles David Gordon of London Street, all of whom were
described as "merchants."[6] These sales reduced the extent to which
Marjoribanks would be injured by the loss of the *Kent*. He was a
man of very considerable means, who was managing owner of no
less than eight Indiamen between 1821 and 1832, six of them during the period of the *Kent*'s last voyage.[7]

As was to be expected of a ship in the service of the greatest of
the British trading companies and making voyages of eighteen
months from the time she cleared London until her return from
Bengal and Canton, and heavily armed for defense and offense, the
Kent was commanded in a highly professional manner. Captain
Cobb had been sworn in on August 9, 1820, and had commanded
Kent on her 1821 voyage to Bombay and Canton, and her 1823
voyage to Bengal and Canton.[8] The regulations that governed his
career, and those of all the *Kent*'s ship's company, were published in
1799 by Charles Hardy in *A Registry of Ships Employed in the
Service of the Honorable East India Company*, which contained a
list of the voyages made to India and China from 1760, with the
names of ship owners and officers. This list was continued to 1835
by his son Horatio Charles A. Hardy.[9] A commanding officer was

The Launch of the Honourable East India Company's Ship Edinburgh by William John Huggins. *Edinburgh* was launched in November 1825 at Blackwell. The top of the mast house at the Brunswick dock is visible behind the ship. (*NMM PAH8417*)

required to be 25 years old, and to have served as first mate for at least one voyage in a company ship, or to have commanded one of the "extra" ships that the company employed under less stringent regulations. As with all the company regulations, these represented an ideal that could be circumvented by influential families. One of the travelers in East India Company ships who has left a memoir of his experiences, William Hickey, tells that his friend, Bob Potts, would have been a commander at the age of 20 had he agreed to his family's expectations.[10] After completing his training as midshipman, Henry Cobb had served in 1813 as second mate of the *Marquis of Huntly*. He had then commanded the 600-ton *Alexander* on her seventh voyage, before taking command of the *Kent*.

The *Kent's* first four mates, the ship's sworn officers, were James Sexton, John Hay, Basil William Muir or Mure, and John

Thomson. Sexton, Hay, and Muir were all on their second voyages on the *Kent*. Sexton had been married on May 25, 1824, to Sarah Briggs, at St. Mary's Newington, in Surrey.[11] One account says that Thomson was the son of the Reverend Mr. Thomson of Duddingston, east of Arthur's Seat in Edinburgh.[12] The *Kent's* fifth and sixth mates were Charles McCray and Mr. Tighe.[13] Company regulations required all mates to have made previous voyages in its service; a fourth mate had to be at least 20 years old, and each step required an additional year of age. The mates all had to "perfect themselves" in the technique for "finding the longitude of a ship at sea by lunar observations." According to Hardy, they were directed to study under Dr. Lawrence Gwynne, at Cambridge House, Hackney, in East London, but it is unclear whether in 1825 that gentleman was still providing instruction.[14] And, as was the case with all sea officers in the age of sail, mates had to understand the rudimentary principles of naval tactics.

Despite being armed, by the beginning of the nineteenth century it was generally understood that Indiamen were not a match for regular warships. But on February 15, 1804, Commodore Nathaniel Dance had shown just how much a well-disciplined fleet of Indiamen could accomplish when the homeward trade from Canton was attacked by a French battle squadron under Rear Admiral Charles-Alexandre Linois. It was truly a nine-days wonder. The Royal Navy generally provided a warship escort for Indiamen in wartime as far south as the island of St. Helena in the South Atlantic ocean, but after that, they were usually obliged to depend on their own resources, sailing in company for mutual support. In the event of coming under attack, the great Indiamen could form a line of battle to give their guns clear arcs of fire, and to provide protection for the smaller company and private "country" ships.

Commodore Dance reported laconically that

At one p.m., finding they purposed to attack and endeavour to
cut off our rear, I made the signal to tack and bear down on him,
and engage in succession—the *Royal George* being the leading
ship, the *Ganges* next, and then the *Earl Camden*. This maneuver was correctly performed, and we stood towards him under a
press of sail. The enemy then formed in a very close line, and
opened their fire on the headmost ships, which was not returned
by us till we approached him nearer. The *Royal George* bore the
brunt of the action, and got as near the enemy as he would permit him. The *Ganges* and *Earl Camden* opened their fire as soon
as their guns could have effect; but before any other ship could
get into action, the enemy hauled their wind, and stood away to
the eastward under all the sail they could set. At two p.m. I made
the signal for a general chase, and we pursued them till four
p.m.; when fearing a longer pursuit would carry us too far from
the mouth of the straits, and considering the immense property
at stake, I made the signal to tack; and at eight p.m. we anchored
in a situation to proceed for the entrance of the straits in the
morning. As long as we could distinguish the enemy, we per-
ceived him steering to the eastward under a press of sail.[15]

The editor of the *Naval Chronicle* crowed that "the signal defeat
of Linois, by a fleet of loaded Merchant Ships, without one Ship of
War in company, is, perhaps, the most complete triumph that
British Sailors have ever enjoyed over the enemies of their country."[16]

In 1825, there was little reason to fear that the *Kent* would be
required to defend herself against warships, but there was always
the danger of piracy. Whatever the danger, or lack of it, the *Kent*
carried a battery of guns. Their weight and length were matters of

constant concern to a company that wanted to transport as much cargo as possible, and by the early nineteenth century the armament of Indiamen was much less than was that of a regular warship of the same size. There is no record of the *Kent*'s armament, but it is known that the *Hindostan* of 1,248 tons carried on its first voyage in 1790 a battery of thirty guns, rated as 12 and 6 pounders.[17] Nominally cannons, these were short guns, with six-foot barrels, as compared to the nine-foot barrels of naval cannon. When in 1795 the *Hindostan* was purchased by the Navy she was classified as a 54-gun, fifth-rate line of battleship.

In 1799, the company permitted owners to arm their ships with relatively shorter and lighter carronades. The *Kent* may have adopted that armament which could fire a heavier ball for its deck weight, but to a relatively short range because of its short barrel.[18] The crews of Indiamen were too small to man the full battery, and it was the usual practice for soldiers being carried as passengers to assist in working the guns. Commodore Dance believed that his fleet would have given the French a hard time had it come to action, but William Hickey recalled in his memoirs that gunnery drill in 1808 in the *Castle Eden* was far from perfect: "Our great guns were now regularly exercised twice a week, though I fear had it been our fate to depend upon the hostile use of them for safety, we should have cut but a wretched bad figure."[19] Hickey made repeated return voyages in Indiamen in the 1760s and 1770s when his dissolute life in London had persuaded his father that the only way to preserve him from disgrace would be to send him out to India as a cadet in the company's service.

The *Kent*'s surgeon was Robert Mackintosh. East India Company regulations required surgeons to have served in one company ship as a surgeon's mate or to have served in the Navy in a hot climate for a year. The company establishment required the employment of a surgeon's mate, and both the surgeon and his mate had to pass examination by the Royal College of Surgeons and by the company's physician, Dr. William Chambers, at 26 Dover Street, Piccadilly.[20]

The company was unique in the mercantile marine in requiring its officers to possess and wear uniforms. The commander and his officers were to "strictly conform to the company's regulations respecting uniforms" and not, "upon any account, appear in boots, or black breeches and stockings." They were required to "appear in your dress uniform when attending the Court of Directors upon any occasion whatever, and in your undress uniform when attending Committees; except on such days when you may be in attendance on the Court of Directors in your dress uniform, and when attending the Council in India, China, or St. Helena." And they were to ensure that their "officers do always appear in their uniforms, when attending the Court of Directors or Committees." The commander's dress uniform was a "blue coat, black velvet lapels, cuffs, and collar, with a light-gold embroidery, as little expensive as may be: waistcoat and breeches deep buff: the buttons yellow metal, with the company's crest, cocked hats, side arms (to be worn under the coat), and black stocks or neckcloths." His undress uniform was a "blue coat, without lapels, black-collar

Uniforms of the commander, left, and first mate in East India service, 1829, by W. Alais. (*NMM PAF0386*)

and cuffs; waistcoat and breeches deep buff, and buttons as above." The mates' uniform was a "blue coat, black velvet lapels, cuffs, and collar: gilt buttons with the company's crest," and with a number of small buttons on their cuffs diminishing from four for the fourth mate to one only for the first mate.[21]

The differences between the officer's rates of pay was relatively small, and the rate of pay low. Commanders were paid £10 a month, the first mate half of that, the second mate £4, the third mate £3/10, and the fourth mate £2/10. Even the purser received £2 per month, and the ship's cook £2, with the captain's cook being paid £3/5.[22] It was not expected that the junior mates would be able to survive on their pay alone. But the £120 Captain Cobb could expect for a year's service, including commanding an immensely valuable ship from London to Bengal and home by way of Canton, was but a small part of the compensation he received. Commanders could claim a fee from the parents of midshipmen and passage money from private passengers, and all officers were permitted to improve their fortune by taking the opportunity to enter into private trade. By the late eighteenth century Indiamen were carrying 100 tons of private cargo for their officers, about half of which was that owned by the commander.

The company tried its best to control these privileges. The commander of company ships was instructed "to cause every package in private trade to be marked with the initials of the name of the person to whom it belongs. They are to be registered with these marks, the nature of the package, the contents, and quality of the contents; nor will any packages marked sundries be permitted to be claimed. . . . Any tea exceeding the value of ten pounds, or any other goods above the value of one hundred pounds, on board the ship unregistered, will be forfeited." The surgeon, who was paid £5 per month, was also permitted six tons of private trade to and from

China, and six from England to India, but only four tons and 32 feet on the homeward voyage. For professional expenses he was also allowed fifteen shillings per man.[23]

But it is certain that these regulations and the government's duties were regularly circumvented. William Hickey was a witness to a transaction that was all too likely routine, and as likely to have been as true in 1825 as it was in 1770 when he made a return voyage from Madras and Canton in the Indiaman *Plassey*. Having weathered a strong northwest gale off the island of Ushant, the *Plassey* had made soundings close to the Lizard Point in Cornwall. There, Hickey remembered, a smuggler was waiting for her.

The 18th [April] we struck soundings in seventy fathoms, and the following morning had the pleasure to see a fine English cutter of one hundred and fifty tons burden within a quarter of a mile of us, from which a man came in a small boat on board the *Plassey*. He was of a Herculean form, with a healthy ruby face. From his dress and appearance I should not have supposed he possessed ten pounds in the world. Captain Waddell conducted him into the round house, where the following short dialogue ensued:

STRANGER: "Well, Captain, how is tea?"

CAPTAIN: "Twenty pounds."

STRANGER: "No, that won't do; eighteen [pounds]—a great number of China ships this season."

CAPTAIN: "Very well, you know best."

STRANGER: "How many chests?"

CAPTAIN: "Sixty odd."

STRANGER: "Come, bear a hand then and get them into the cutter."

By this I found our new visitor was a smuggler. The foregoing was all that passed in completing the sale and purchase of so large a quantity of tea. In the same laconic manner he bought the stock of the different officers. . . .

This was well beyond the quota for the private sale of tea permitted the Company officers, and the Crown Revenue officers were required to try and stop the transaction. Hickey continued:

A thick haze that had prevailed all the morning just then cleared away, and we saw the land (the Lizard) not more than four leagues distant. The cutter at the same time hailed to inform their chief they saw the Albert (custom-house schooner) to the southward.

"Do you, by God," replied he, and taking a spying glass from one of the officers, looked through it in the direction pointed out, directly saying, "Aye, aye, sure enough there she comes and under a cloud of canvas." Turning to Captain Waddell, he continued, "Come, Captain, you must haul off the land another league or so, and then let him fetch us with all my heart, and kiss my a—e."

Captain Waddell appearing to hesitate as to complying, the man hastily said, "He can seize me at this distance from our coast. If, therefore, you don't stand further off, I must leave you."

Captain Waddell then desired the officer of the watch to brace the yards and keep the ship up a couple of points, which being done, in an hour and a half the smuggler said: "Now, Captain, let them come and be damned, you may keep your course again."

The schooner was then within two miles, and in another hour came dashing by close to us in a noble style, and hove to upon our weather bow, when a most capital exchange of naval blackguardism took place between the smuggler's crew and the schooner, continuing a full hour; but, as the *Plassey* was then beyond the stated limits, they could not molest the cutter, and remained only to have the mortification of seeing a large quantity of goods transferred from the ship to her. At length they sheered off, when the smuggler observed: "The fellow that commands her is one of the damnedest scoundrels that lives, and the only rascal amongst them that I cannot deal with, though I have bid roundly too." (I do not remember the name of this extraordinary revenue officer, or I would mention it, as, I am afraid, a rare instance of integrity in his line.)

The smuggler then completed the transaction by paying Captain Waddell, by cheque, £1,224.[24]

Apart from the six mates and surgeon, the complement of a ship of the size of the *Kent* was required to include a caulker, and a cooper, each with his mate, the two cooks, each with a steward, a boatswain, a carpenter, and a gunner, each with two mates, six quarter-masters, a sailmaker, a purser, a master-at-arms, a midshipman, and coxswain, four other midshipmen, an armorer, a butcher, a baker, a poulterer, eight servants for the senior officers (the commander, who had two, the first and second mates, the surgeon, boatswain, gunner and carpenter), and 78 foremast men. The gunner and gunner's mate had to be certified by the company's master-attendant.[25] The total complement was supposed to be 130 men, but MacGregor tells us that there were 148 on the ship leaving the Downs. It was also permitted to sign on five supernumeraries, but only two of these were to be permitted "to walk the quarter-deck."[26]

No other merchant service provided its ships with this number of technical tradesmen, and their pay was considered to be very good, even though it had scarcely changed for over a century. Even foremast hands were paid between £2 and £3 per month, plus their food and accommodation. The company also paid anyone losing a limb in defending its interests a sum of £30 with a guaranteed shore job in the warehouses on Cutler Street, and the company maintained a retirement home at Poplar in East London. Two months pay was advanced before ships left Gravesend, and men could arrange for one month's pay every six months to be given to their dependents ashore. The least satisfactory aspect of their wages was that no British shipowner was required to pay any arrears should a crew fail to bring its ship safely into port with its cargo intact.[27] *Kent*'s crew were to be faced with that reality.

Because of the competition for seamen to supply the crews for other trades, and for the Navy, manning East Indiamen for the long voyages to and from Asia was always difficult. Disease often dramatically thinned the crew before it reached Asia, although the provision of lemon or lime juice reduced that problem. In the seventeenth century the East India Company surgeon John Woodall had recommended the use of lemon juice as a preventive and cure of scurvy in his book, *Surgeon's Mate*.[28] More than a hundred years later, in 1747, the Royal Navy surgeon James Lind undertook what is regarded as the first controlled dietary experiment ever made by providing lemon juice for part of a ship's crew, but it was 1795 before the Royal Navy adopted lemon or lime juice as standard issue at sea.

Once a ship reached an African or Asian port desertion could be a problem. In wartime, manning difficulties could become extreme because of the very real danger of a navy captain, hungry for hands, sending a press gang on board. As a result, the company had come to depend on recruiting Chinese and South Asian sailors, known as Lascars, for the homeward voyage, on a ratio of three to one English sailor. When Hickey returned home in the *Castle Eden* in 1808, he described the crew as "motley, consisting of natives of almost every nation of Europe, besides nine Americans and eighteen Chinese. Certainly we had not more than ten English seamen on board." They also had 18 French prisoners of war: "Of these eighteen French the majority were as desperate and ill-looking rascals as ever I beheld, nor should I have felt at all at my ease with such a set of fellows and such a crew as we had on board, had we been a single ship or sailing without convoy."[29] At that time, the word "convoy" was used to refer to a warship escort.

After the end of the Napoleonic war it might have been expected that the crew situation would have improved, but that does not necessarily mean that the company was able to attract the best of men. One who joined the company's service because he was desperate for work was the marine painter Clarkson Stanfield who had been invalided out of the navy after suffering a debilitating fall. He signed on the crew list of the *Warley* East Indiaman in March 1815 for a voyage to China, from which he returned the following May. Pages from a journal Stanfield kept during this time, and a sketchbook dated July 24, 1815, are filled with pictures of China and the Philippines.[30] He turned to theater set painting in July 1816 when his next ship, the Indiaman *Hope*, failed to sail for Madras.

By an act of parliament in the fourth year of the reign of George IV, Chapter 80 of 1823, it was ruled that the company had to employ four English sailors for every hundred tons, but it was a council of perfection that might not reflect reality. Because of the provisions of the Navigation Act, which was intended to encourage the growth of the British merchant marine, Asian sailors could not be employed on the outward voyage, and had to be transported as passengers. But it does not appear that there were any onboard the *Kent*, probably because all the deck space would be needed for the regiment. What was to become clear, however, was that *Kent*'s crew were not of the best.

T HE task of preparing an Indiaman, such as the *Kent*, for sea was vast, but had become a routine. After the return cargo from China had been landed, the ship would have been overhauled, which included putting her into the East India Export Dock so that the bottom could be surveyed and any weaknesses repaired. By 1825, company ships were all plated with copper under the waterline to prevent shipworms from boring into the hull and to discourage marine growth in general; as a result, voyage times were considerably shorter than they had been in the mid-eighteenth century before copper plating came into use. Any damage to the copper following a voyage had to be repaired, and iron fittings had to be inspected to insure that they had not been corroded as a result of electrolytic action.

The East India Export Dock had been built between March 1805 and August 1806 at Blackwall, near the ship-building slips.[31] Originally known as Brunswick Dock and forming part of John Perry's shipyard, in 1806 the dock had been bought by the East India Dock Company. Two years later an Import Dock was built next to it with a separate entrance beyond Perry's basin. Towering over the Indiamen fitting out in the dock was a mast house with a crane that was capable of lifting the massive masts and a bowsprit into a ship in less than four hours.

Unless the tide was exceptionally high, a fully laden ship could not safely cross the sill of the dock gate, and would have to be partly unloaded into lighters in the stream or in the basin that provided access between the river and the dock. Therefore, it was stipulated that

> In order to prevent heavy loss that would arise by accidents to ships fully laden coming into the said docks, or to provide as much as possible for such events, should it happen, as well as to

The Mast House and Brunswick Dock at Blackwall by William Daniell. This facility was purhased by the East India Dock Company in 1806. (*NMM BHC1867*)

render the basin and locks less crowded with ships or craft, and the crews within the dock premises from being longer therein than is requisite for the safety of their respective vessels, it is ordained, that no ship shall be admitted within the dock or basin gates, unless in cases of emergency, that is not dismantled to her lower masts, and her guns, ammunition, anchors, and stores delivered, in such extent as the Dock Master shall prescribe.[32]

Once the hull was ready for sea, company regulations stipulated that the commander present his "four sworn officers for the approbation of the Committee of Shipping, previous to your ship coming afloat; and not any part of the company's cargo will be sent on board your ship, until all those officers shall have been examined and approved by that Committee, and sworn in before the Court of Directors."

In the spring of 1825, the committee was chaired by Mr. William Astell, who was Chairman of the Court of Directors at the time and held that position four times, in 1810–11, 1824–25, 1828–29, and 1830–31. His deputy, Campbell Marjoribanks, was a close relative of the owner of the *Kent*. He had been Chairman of the Court between 1819 and 1820, and was to be again in 1825–26 and 1833–34.[33]

The ship's stores could begin to be brought on board when only one of the mates had been sworn. But to assist him and ensure regulations were complied with, the company would send its surveyor on board on the day it was planned to float the ship, or on the first day of the spring tide. The chief or first mate had to sign a customs bond for the stores, for which purpose he had to seek the assistance of Mr. Robert Gear, the Company's Husband, or his assistant, John Foster, and from the time stores began coming on board he or the second mate had to remain on the ship at all times.[34]

An important consideration behind the construction of the docks was that the ships and warehouses could be kept secure behind the dockyard wall and gates. The East India Company had its warehouses at Cutler Street, near the City of London, about four miles away; nevertheless, the docks provided security against pilfering, and company regulations forbade access to the docks by any but the ship's sworn officers or the king's officers and dockyard officials, and none of those were permitted inside the gates after 4 p.m. It was estimated in the *Civil Engineer and Architect's Journal* of 1849, that "before the construction of the great docks, the loss by robberies alone exceeded the hundreth part of the whole importation of wines, tea, indigo, cocoa, &c.; the fiftieth of the sugar, and the fortieth of the rum. The value of the loss during the years 1799, 1800, 1801, was estimated at £1,214,500."[35]

Charles Hardy included in his *Registry* a list of the stores that would have been laded into the *Kent*. At the top of the list for a 1,200 ton or larger East Indiaman were 13 1/2 tons of ale, beer,

wine, or other liquors in casks or bottles, for the use of the commander's table, allowing 252 gallons, or 83 dozen quart bottles to
the ton. The provision for the remaining crewmen was an additional 26 tons of beer and 10 puncheons of brandy or other spirits. The
ship also carried 260 pounds each of essence of malt, and essence
of spruce, for brewing beer once the original provision was
exhausted. East India commanders lived well! But voyages were
long and the stores for his table also had to provide for all the senior officers and passengers. The previous two voyages by the *Kent*,
to Bombay and Bengal, respectively, each returning by way of
Canton, had taken over 18 and 15 months. Each stage could last up
to six months.

Food and amenities included: beef, pork, bacon, suet, and
tongues—40 tons; bread—350 hundredweight; butter—30 firkins;
cheese—50 hundredweight; confectionary—6 cones; flour—134
hundredweight; fish—21 hundredweight; lime or lemon juice—130
gallons; mustard seed—10 bushels; oatmeal—50 bushels, with
another 500 bushels of oats, barley, and bran; oranges and
lemons—6 chests; peas—200 bushels; potatoes—15 tons; red and
white herrings & salmon—5 barrels; tobacco—30 hundredweight;
vinegar—11 hogsheads; and water—70 tons. The water was drawn
directly out of the river Thames at Gravesend, and stank, but fer-
mentation eventually disposed of the organic matter, rendering the
water healthier than was that for the return voyage, drawn from the
Hooghly River downstream from Calcutta.[36] The water would
have been used in cooking, but for drinking, passengers and crew
depended on beer as long, as it lasted, wine, and spirits. By bread
was meant hard biscuit, virtually inedible unless soaked; confectionary was sugar pressed into cones; fish was stockfish, meaning
sun-flaked Norwegian hake or haddock and distinguished from
smoked and salted herring (red and white herring) and salmon. The

10 bushels of mustard seed were probably sprouted and eaten as an additional means of preventing scurvy.

No distinction was made between edible oil and lamp oil, it merely being determined that a total of 300 gallons was required for the voyage. In 1825, Sarah Speedy's mother saved a company ship from a serious fire that she believed had been caused by the second mate becoming intoxicated and putting turpentine in the lamps instead of lamp oil.[37]

Indiamen being fully armed for self-defense, the *Kent* was laded with 65 barrels of gunpowder, and 6 tons of iron shot. For cooking and light, she carried 25,000 billets of wood of a standard size to fit the cooking stove, 20 chaldrons of coal, each measuring 36 bushels, and 20 dozen candles. And for maintenance were laded canvas—30 bolts; iron—6 tons; oilman's stores—3 cases; spare cordage—7 tons; tar—20 barrels; and turpentine—3 barrels. Two chests of slops, or seamen's clothing, were also carried to be sold by the purser. All were checked onboard by the managing owner's agent, known as the ship's "husband," or by the sealers at the East India wharfs lining the dockside whose job was to check and put seals on cargo containers. The only exception was that the lading of the commander's liquor store was supervised by the company's husband.

Before the commander would be permitted to take his leave of the Court of Directors he and the first mate had to swear that enough lemons had been taken aboard to provide for the crew on the outward voyage, enough deals (wooden boards used to keep cargo from shifting) had been put into the hold to ensure the safe storage of the return cargo, with enough water, and the required amounts of wet and dry provisions.[38] The chests of fresh oranges and lemons would have been used up early in the voyage, after which the puncheons of juice would be broached.

The *Kent*'s purser, William E. Browne, assumed responsibility for the stores, but James Sexton, the first mate, would have seen to their stowage. This was a difficult and important task, as the placement of stores had to be determined by their weight as well as by the need to be able to reach them at sea when the purser decided to serve them out. When the cargo was brought onboard the same considerations of weight and stowage applied, with others concerned with the protection of the cargo and the liability of the company. It had been shown by the French mathematician Pierre Bouguer, in 1746, that the stability of a ship is quantifiable, by measuring the distance its "metacenter" is above its center of gravity, having first located the metacenter at the point of intersection of two vertical lines drawn through the center of buoyancy when the ship is upright, and when it is healed over.[39] The distance between the ship's center of gravity and its metacenter, known as the metacentric height, determines both the stability of the ship, and the extent and period of its roll. The placement of cargo and stores was a matter of great importance and difficulty. If the heaviest hogsheads (casks usually used for wines and spirits) were placed too high in the hold, the ship could become unstable. But if they were stowed far below the metacenter, the roll would be exaggerated, and could be dangerous. The difficulty of placing the weights correctly was exacerbated by the problem of supporting the heaviest items. All too often they would have to be stowed on the bottom of the hold. Elaborate instructions were given for the storage of copper sheets, which were heavy but liable to damage from humidity and salt. All of the barrels and hogsheads had to be chocked so that they would not move when the ship rolled. Any miscalculation could be fatal. And it was when the *Kent* developed a heavy roll and one of the spirit barrels broke loose and was stove in, that her fate was sealed.

Particular care was also to be taken on the return voyage for the safe handling of delicate cargo, such as coral heads, which were both expensive and liable to damage if they were stowed where their packaging could become damp, and the knots holding them rotted. Military stores also had to be protected from damp, and a description of their contents had to be provided by the Inspector of Military Stores. The company's own chests of arms had to be protected from damage when they were being brought aboard, and some of them had to be kept handy for defensive purposes. *Kent*'s cargo included 100 tons of lead, valued at £2,169/10/1, and stores for the civil government of Bengal valued at £1,043/10/17. MacGregor said there was "some hundred" tons of ammunition onboard, but that might have been the iron shot in the ship's stores, or the lead that was listed in the accounts and which might have been intended for molding into musket balls.[40] The great weight of these items of cargo made lading difficult, and would have contributed to the heavy roll the *Kent* developed at sea.

Even while a ship was being stored, priority was given to loading the company's cargo when it came alongside in lighters: "that if it appear that any craft shall have been unnecessarily detained, the commanding officer will be charged with the amount of the demurrage arising from such detention." But an even higher priority was given to stores "for His Majesty's services in the East Indies." That was to be loaded on board as soon as it appeared alongside, unless His Majesty's recruits were at the time coming onboard, or the ship was taking onboard any bullion.[41] This provision would have come into force when the 31st Regiment came onboard the *Kent* at Gravesend.

Once the hull was ready for sea, the stores and part of the cargo laded, the ship would be brought into the basin to have her upper masts, spars, guns, ammunition, and anchors put back onboard, and then she would be brought down river to Gravesend to complete her cargo where the water was deeper. The commander and mates were required to be onboard for that passage, and the commander had to come onboard at least once a week when the ship was completing its lading. When all was ready for sea, he then had to visit the company headquarters to take his leave of the Court of Directors and certify that the ship had cleared customs. At the same time, the company surveyor had to certify that the officers were onboard. The ship's journal, and the surgeon's log, were sent onboard and the commander was on two days' notice to board his ship, and start her on her passage. In the *Kent*'s case, this would be her last.

Although he may have worked from sketches made at an earlier time, the ship portrait of the *Kent* painted by William Huggins, dated 1825, shows her hove to in the Downs with her main topsail backed to pick up the pilot for the passage down Channel on her final voyage. Huggins certainly knew his subject. He had been steward and assistant purser in the East India Company ship *Perseverance*, and it is known that he sailed in her to Bombay and Calcutta in December 1812, returning in August 1814. He had then left the sea and set himself up as a marine painter in Leadenhall Street near the East India Company offices. His output was prodigious and his work was popular with seamen, including King William IV who had served in the Royal Navy. (*Vallejo Maritime Gallery, Newport Beach, California*)

Departure

ON DECEMBER 8, 1824, CAPTAIN COBB was sworn in to command the *Kent* for her third voyage, and on January 27th, the Court of Directors placed a notice in the *Times* that the day before he and several other commanders had taken leave of the court "previous to departing for their respective destinations."[1] The last entry in a receipt book was dated February 1st, showing payments to the ship's officers and perhaps to some of the foredeck hands from December 27, 1824, after which Captain Cobb presumably deposited it at East India House.[2]

From that time on none of the ship's sworn officers was to leave the *Kent*, except for short emergencies. For some reason, however, the surgeon and surgeon's mate did not have to come onboard until the ship was in the Hope Reach three miles east of Tilbury Fort, the last sheltered anchorage inside the Thames River. Company regulations enjoined officers to be watchful that recruits did not desert on the way down river, or find an opportunity to sell their company issue clothing for alcohol. Any boats being towed alongside had to be locked with a chain to prevent the recruits from using them to effect their escape.[3]

The company strictly controlled who could travel on its ships to and from India. The Charter Act of 1813 stipulated that no one could travel out to India as a writer who had not spent four terms in Haileybury College.[4] In January 1824, a number of the directors wanted to petition parliament to have that regulation changed and replaced with a requirement for a public examination of the candidate, but a majority voted against.[5] In the company's regulations it was stipulated that "a commander who shall carry out or bring home any passenger or person without the leave of the Court of Directors . . . shall forfeit the following sums, in addition to the penalty in the charter-party, viz: For a male or female black servant, being a native of India or other country, the sum of twenty pounds. For an European, or for a native of India, being the child of an European, five hundred pounds."[6] The original rationale for this control was to prevent merchants who were not part of the monopoly company, known as Interlopers, from using the company transport in order to enter into illegal business in India. But the company also had other practical considerations in mind. Should permission be given for a passenger to transport to England a "black," i.e. an Indian servant, a bond was to be collected to defray the cost of returning the servant to India should he or she ever be discharged from service. Nor did the company want Europeans in India who would complicate its relationship with the local rulers. One of the provisions of the the Charter Act of 1813 was that for the first time missionaries were permitted to join the merchants and soldiers in British India.

Regulations forbade that "any female persons, either relatives or others, do accompany yourself, or any of your officers, petty officers, or seamen, on board your ship, on her passage from Gravesend to the Downs or Portsmouth." Like all such rules, that one may sometimes have been breached. Male visitors, however, did certainly make the relatively short passage to the Downs. One such was John Constable the landscape painter. In the spring of 1803 when he was 27 years old and a student at the Royal Academy of Arts, he made the 75-mile trip down the Thames and around the corner to Deal. This was to lead to his only effort at painting a naval subject. The voyage took a month, including the time spent at Gravesend making final preparations for the voyage to China. While his ship was taking onboard the last of its cargo at Gravesend he decided to walk across the Cooling marshes to the Medway.

> When the ship was at Gravesend, I took a walk on shore to Rochester and Chatham. Their situation is beautiful and romantic, being at the bottom of finely formed and high hills, with the river continually showing its turnings to great advantage. Rochester Castle is one of the most romantic I ever saw. At Chatham I hired a boat to see the men of war, which are there in great numbers. I sketched the *Victory* in three views. She was the flower of the flock, a three decker of (some say) 112 guns. She looked very beautiful fresh out of Dock and newly painted. When I saw her they were bending the sails; which circumstance, added to a very fine evening, made a charming effect. . . . I joined the ship again at Gravesend, and we proceeded on our voyage, which was pleasant enough till we got out to sea, when we were joined by three more ships. We had almost reached the Downs when the weather became stormy, and we all put back under the North Foreland, and lay there three days. Here I saw some very grand effects of stormy clouds. I came on shore at Deal, walked to Dover, and the next day returned to London. The worst part of the story is that I have lost all my drawings. The ship was such a scene of confusion, when I left her, that although I had done my drawings up very carefully, I left them behind. When I found,

on landing, that I had left them, and saw the ship out of reach, I was ready to faint.[7]

The sketch book was eventually recovered, and he was able to use those of the *Victory* three years later when he decided to paint a picture of the battle of Trafalgar in which the *Victory* had served as Vice-Admiral Lord Nelson's flagship.[8]

Ten years after the end of the war against Napoleon, the *Kent* was to transport the right wing of the 31st Regiment commanded by Lieutenant Colonel Robert Bryce Fearon, and the regimental headquarters, to Bengal. There it was to join the left wing to form the garrison at Calcutta. The tragic story of the loss of the *Kent* is therefore an important part of the regiment's history.[9]

The 31st, also designated the Huntington Regiment, had been formed in 1702 as a Marine Corps, and had proved itself a crack force. It had done notable service in the war declared in 1793 by the French republic, until the final defeat of Emperor Napoleon in 1815.[10] In the first campaign, it had formed part of the allied force in Flanders under the incompetent command of the "Grand Old" Duke of York, second son of King George III, with its flank companies going to fight in the West Indies. The regiment later joined them there under the command of Sir Ralph Abercrombie. In 1799, it formed part of the expeditionary force commanded again by the Duke of York in the Netherlands, under the immediate command of the no less incompetent Earl of Chatham, brother of William Pitt, but with Abercrombie in superior command. After the collapse of that abortive campaign, the 31st was scheduled to take part in an assault into Quiberon Bay, which was cancelled, and then went as part of Abercrombie's force to the Mediterranean. The battalion spent five frustrating months onboard transports, and then served at Malta, Minorca, and Jersey.

A second battalion was formed in 1805. It obtained battle honors at Talavera in 1809 and in 1811 at Albuera, where it suffered heavily from Marshal Soult's Polish cavalry charging home in a hail storm; but the 31st steadily formed square under fire and drove off the enemy. Later it provided the means of extricating the army from a bloody deadlock, making a bayonet charge in which 155 men were lost out of 398. In a desperate counter-attack in 1813, Major General John Byng grabbed the regimental colors as he led the divisional assault. He was so impressed by the conduct of the regiment that he asked its colonel, the Earl of Mulgrave, whether a representation of the colors could be incorporated into his family's coat of arms. With the exile of Napoleon to Elba the second battalion was disbanded.[11]

Uniform of the 31st Regiment of Foot, 1825. The cockade was white and red, the coat red with white facings, and the trousers blue. (*Author*)

Colonel Fearon had been born at Quebec April 2, 1783, and been commissioned ensign in the 88th Foot on November 12, 1794, when he was only 11 years old. He transferred into the 31st Regiment as a lieutenant on September 4, 1795, and suffered a pike or bayonet wound in the knee at the battle of La Vigie in 1797. He may also have been wounded at the battle of Rosetta.[12]

After service at Belfast and then Dublin, the regiment was transferred by sea to Portsmouth in the summer of 1824, preparatory to being sent to India, and went into quarters at Gosport.[13] On

January 12, 1825, it marched to Chatham, in Kent county, where it arrived eight days later, ready to embark at Gravesend on the lower Thames. The regiment could not all be accommodated in a single ship, and it was ordered that the right wing and headquarters were to travel in the *Kent*, while the left wing was to travel in the *Scaleby Castle*, a teak-built Indiaman launched in Bombay in 1798.[14] It would have been well for the *Kent* and the people in her had the two Indiamen kept together through the voyage.

The men of the 31st Regiment with their wives and children took the same road John Constable had taken, and marched from their barracks at Chatham to join the *Kent* at Gravesend. On board, they slept on the main gun deck, or in bunks three high in the orlop deck below the waterline. Ordinarily the number of wives of "other ranks"—those married with permission and entitled to draw rations—was limited to six per company, which in February 1821 had been set at 72 rank and file. But the *Kent* was officially carrying thirteen more women than the usual allowance, plus the officers' wives, and there was at least one stowaway. MacGregor tells us that the wife of one "respectable" man "to whom he was warmly attached" hid onboard at Gravesend. "She ingeniously managed, by eluding the vigilance of the sentries, to get on board, and conceal herself for several days." She was discovered and sent ashore at Deal while the *Kent* was waiting a wind in the Downs, but "she contrived a second time, with true feminine perseverance, to get within decks, were she continued to secrete herself until the morning of the fatal disaster."[15] Her name is unknown, and the names of the wives of privates and non-commissioned officers would be entirely lost, but for the death of the wife of Sergeant William Molloy in the fire, the witness statement of Mary Healy who was the daughter of a private, and the tragedy that was to befall Anne, wife of Sergeant James Curry or Currie. She was

Minerva, left, *Scaleby Castle*, center, and the *Charles Grant*, right, off Cape Town, South Africa, painted by Thomas Whitcombe in 1820. *Scaleby Castle* was destined to carry the left wing of the 31st Regiment, while the *Kent* carried the right. The *Charles Grant* would ultimately transport most of the right wing of the 31st to India following the loss of the *Kent*. (*NMM BHC3492*)

obliged to petition the Governor of Chatham, Sir Archibald Christie, for a letter of reference, and he described her as "an honest, industrious, painstaking, woman [who] has at all times conducted herself during the times her husband served in the 31st Regiment in an exemplary manner by bring up her family morally and creditably."[16]

Duncan MacGregor's name was on the *Kent*'s passenger list because he was commissioned in the right wing of the first, and at the time, the only battalion of the 31st Regiment. MacGregor had been born March 16, 1787, the son of John MacGregor of the family of Learan in Rannoch. On July 12, 1800 at the age of thirteen, he was commissioned an ensign in the 72nd Regiment, promoted lieutenant on August 31, 1801, and captain in the 78th on April 17, 1804. It is probable that, as was common in the British army at the time, he purchased these commissions.[17] MacGregor served in Sicily and Italy in 1806 and was shot through the right shoulder at the battle of Maida. He took part in the campaigns in Egypt in 1807, in the disastrous Walcheren expedition in 1809, and after four years recruiting at Aberdeen, served in the Netherlands. Being promoted a brevet major in the 78th on November 25, 1813, he served in the Peninsular campaign in 1813–14 and at the capture of Corsica in May 1814. Following the conclusion of peace, he transferred to the 31st Regiment then stationed in Ireland.[18] At 37 years, he was well launched on a military career that was to last until his 90th year.

According to MacGregor, when the *Kent* left the Downs, the sheltered anchorage inside the Goodwin Sands in the English Channel, on February 19th, she had onboard "20 officers, 344 soldiers, 43 women, and 66 children, belonging to the 31st Regiment; with 20 private passengers, and a crew (including officers) of 148 men on board." The 66 children in MacGregor's list must all have been those of the women accompanying "other ranks" because those of the officer's wives were counted as private passengers.

As was appropriate in a class-conscious age, the colonel's wife's name led the list of passengers later published in the *Times*.[19] Mrs. Fearon, née Mary Palmer, had married her husband on September 15, 1821 at the fashionable church of St. George's Hanover Square on St. James's Street in Westminster.[20] At that time, Colonel Fearon had given his address as the parish of Charles, in Plymouth, Devon, and it appears that his wife lived in the St. George's parish before she was married. She was accompanied by five girls. The eldest three, Margaret-Eliza born October 23, 1808, Henrietta Jane born August 1, 1812, and Mary Anne born December 9, 1813, were from Colonel Fearon's earlier marriage to Eliza Perrot, who had died at Malta in 1816. Mary had given birth to three children in the three and a half years since her marriage to Robert; Frederica Eliza born August 24, 1822, Charlotte Anne Beacon born on February 15, 1824, and Frederick George William born on February 9th, only ten days before the *Kent* sailed.[21] There is no record whether he was onboard, but he may have been as babies were not often recorded on passenger lists.

Portrait of Lieutenant Colonel (later General) Sir Duncan MacGregor, KCB, by Sir John Watson Gordon. (*Argyle and Sutherland Museum*)

Mrs. MacGregor, second on the list, had been born Elizabeth Douglas Trotter, the daughter of Sir William Dick, Baronett, of Prestonfield.[22] She married Duncan on March 19, 1824, and her infant son was born on January 24th while his parents were waiting to go on board the *Kent* at Gravesend. Elizabeth was so weak after giving birth that there was some uncertainty about whether she could accompany her husband to India, so she did not go onboard before the *Kent* sailed from Gravesend. But at the last minute, her sister, Joanna Dick, announced that she would accompany her. With Joanna's support and that of her cousin David Pringle, who was traveling to India as a company writer, she felt able to undertake the voyage. On February 18th, Elizabeth was transferred onboard a comfortable yacht by a small boat, into which had been placed her invalid cot, for the voyage out of the Thames to the Downs where the *Kent* was waiting for an easterly wind to take her down Channel. She was then hoisted up the high sides of the *Kent* and placed in a sofa-bed. For the first night before leaving English waters, she continued to be attended by her physician, Dr. Deaumont, and by her nurse.

Elizabeth's son was to go by the name of John in adult life, but
as a baby he was given the nickname of Rob Roy after a robber
ancestor. His biographer says that his healthy lungs added to the tur-
moil onboard. Elizabeth was distressed when she came on deck as
they passed down Channel to see the bodies of two soldiers' babies
who had died being committed to the sea, but her own son proved
to be remarkably resilient.23 It was indeed little short of miraculous
that he and any of the children onboard the *Kent* survived.

Elizabeth MacGregor's voyage to the Downs in a yacht was
unusual, but passengers did often shorten their stay on board by
traveling by coach from London to Deal, and boarding the ship in
the Downs. It is probable that some if not all the Kent's passengers
spared themselves the often uncomfortable and tedious passage out
of the Thames and joined her at Deal.

Six of the passengers signed a letter of thanks following their rescue: David Pringle, Elizabeth MacGregor's cousin, James Grant,
three cadets in the company's army H. Shuckburgh, B. Birch, J.
Hatchetts, and Edward R. Townsend M.D. As Dr. Townsend's
name is missing from the passenger list published by the *Times*, it
must be supposed that he was serving on board in his professional
capacity, although his appointment as assistant surgeon in the company's service may have been for a shore post in India. We know a
little about James Grant, who was employed in the Bengal Civil
Service as a writer. We know this because the official papers he was
carrying out to India had to be recopied following the loss of his
portmanteau in the *Kent*. He asked the Board to have that done for
him at its expense.24

Of the other passengers it is possible that the "A Shaw" shown
in the *Times*' list as an ensign was the W. A. Shaw who had first
gone out to India in 1811 and had established an extensive indigo

business in Bhangulpoor. He had then wished to return to England, for which purpose he had had to conform to the company's control of the right to travel to and from India. On the strength of a letter from Secretary Lushington, that "government is satisfied with Mr. Shaw's conduct during the period he has resided in this country," he was given permission to travel home in the *Ganges* in June 1824. But he had quickly decided that the prosperity of his business depended on his immediate return to Bengal. In January, he had written to Joseph Dart, the secretary to the company Court of Directors, requesting permission to travel back in the *Kent*.[25]

Captain Bray, having transferred into the 31st Regiment, was returning to India after having served with the 67th Regiment through the Maharatta Campaign of 1817 and 1818 and at the siege and capture of Amulnair, Ryghur, and Asseeghur. With him were his wife Belinda, who was twenty-seven years old, and two infant sons.[26] Of the other women listed in the *Times*, Miss Catherine Murray was the Brays' friend. A "Mrs Waters" was probably the wife of the quartermaster.

Apart from Lieutenant Colonel Fearon, Major MacGregor, Captain Bray, and the three cadets, 17 other officers appeared on the passenger list: Captains Sir Charles Farrington, Bart., R. T. Green, James Spence, Lieutenant Charles Shaw who was serving as the regimental Adjutant, Lieutenants George Baldwin, D. B. T. Dodgin, George Ruxton, William Booth, A. Douglas, R. Campbell, Edmund Gennys, Ensigns Thomas Tait, Asaph Shaw, H. Evans, Assistant Surgeon Edward Graham, Quarter-Master J. W. Waters, and Paymaster R. Monk. The *Times* gave Dodgin's name as Badger, and Gennys as Gulanis.[27]

On July 11, 1810, under the watchful eye of the Board of Control and its chairman the secretary of state, the company court of directors had laid down the maximum amount that could be charged officers for passage. Otherwise, unscrupulous ship captains would supplement their income by making exorbitant charges. General officers in the company army, for instance, could not be charged more than £250 for a passage from England to India, and army captains could be charged no more than £125. Civilian writers en route to India were charged £110, and cadets no more than £25. The senior officers and their wives, of course, would get the most comfortable accommodation, and also eat at the commander's table. Cadets did not always rate that privilege, but could be entertained at the third mate's table, at an additional cost, although the mate was "restrained from demanding more than the sum of £55, for the accommodation of an assistant surgeon or cadet, who may proceed in their mess to India." The company subsidized the accommodation of cadets at the rate of three shillings and sixpence per day at the commander's table, and two shillings and sixpence at the third mate's table.

The officers of the 31st Regiment were charged a lower rate. General officers in the king's service could be charged no more than £235, colonels £135, and subalterns and assistant surgeons £25; but the company also paid a charter party payment to the ship owner for all of them. To prevent demands for under the table payments by the third mate or by the commander should a junior officer be accepted at his table, it was stipulated that the payments for passage by the lower ranks should be made "to the paymaster of seaman's wages; and the order for the reception of any persons, in either of those stations, on board any of the ships in the company's service, shall not be delivered, until they shall have produced the paymaster's receipt." Even more control was imposed on the return voyage, with commanders being required to receive onboard two junior officers trying to get home. Without that provision, the space

"An interesting scene on board an East Indiaman, showing the Effects of a heavy Lurch after dinner," an 1818 engraving after George Cruikshank. While the cartoon is comical, it accurately portrays both the layout of the great cabin, including the guns, and the disruption of heavy rolling. (*British Library*)

would certainly have been given over to private passengers able to pay a higher rate.[28]

Space for passengers was usually limited to the great cabin across the stern, to the officer's cabins forward of it which might be available, and to the round house and cuddy on a level with the quarter deck. The cuddy was the lobby in which the passengers dined at the commander's table.[29] The cabins were contrived by canvas screens, with "canvas births [*sic*] only, laced down to battens on the deck, with upright stanchions, one cross-piece, and a small door, with canvas panels, . . . the battens do not exceed one inch square, nor the stanchions or cross-pieces two inches square each; and that the births be made with panels, and the canvass to roll up." Similar screens were used in the great cabin and round house to provide a degree of privacy. Passengers in the great cabin complained of the dreadful smells below decks, and the noises from children in the cabin and the adjoining steerage. Those in the round house and cuddy complained that their rest was broken by the noise made by sailors working on the deck above.[30] No partitions or cabins were permitted in the steerage or before the bulk-head of the great cabin.

Because of the crowding, and the money to be made by the commander by squeezing in as many passengers as possible, there was a temptation to build additional cabins on deck, or to subdivide those below it. "Should you be desirous (in the event of a number of passengers proceeding in your ship) to build a cabin not exceeding seven feet on each side of the deck, an application must be made to the Committee for that purpose."[31] These restrictions reflected the fact that East India Company ships were warships equipped with full gun batteries, and might need to clear away the cabins in short order so as to work the guns. Passengers were expected to bring their own furniture with them, and to take it with them on reaching India.

The Downs anchorage between Ramsgate and Dover, inside the Goodwin Sands, was virtually a floating city in the early nineteenth century, with ships waiting for a wind to go down Channel or to northern ports. It was customary for passengers of Indiamen to live ashore at an inn while the ship waited for a favorable easterly wind, but they had to be ready for immediate departure as soon as the commander fired a warning gun. Hickey wrote that he and some friends "had passed a very merry day, and were just talking of going to bed when we heard a gun fired, and soon after several others from different ships in the Downs. A Deal man coming in told us the wind had suddenly gone to the north-east, and the fleet were getting under weigh. Instead, therefore, of retiring to our comfortable beds, we were obliged to prepare for embarking. In a few min-

A contemporary map of Kent County showing Gravesend just across the Thames from Tilbury, located at top left. Ships would travel to the Downs, located along the east coast just north of Dover, on the right, where they would wait for favorable winds to take them down Channel and out to the open ocean. It was not uncommon for passengers to bypass the trip to the Downs and take an overland trip from London to Deal on the Channel coast where they would then meet the ship and embark.

utes the house was all hurry and confusion—paying bills, packing trunks, etc. etc. . . . . It was a bleak night, blowing smartly, with snow.[32] He found that his foresight in making a contract with one of the watermen to take him off at a fixed rate paid off. The ship would wait for no one.

As the *Kent's* log was not recovered from the wreck we do not know the time of day she raised her anchor and cleared the Downs, although the fact that Captain Bray told his friend that the *Kent* sailed on the 20th indicates it must have been before noon. He would have been using the civil calendar, whereas the ship would have been using the nautical calendar that runs from noon to noon.[33] When the *Scaleby Castle* sailed the same day it was late enough that her log mentions sighting the "South Foreland Lights WNW 6 miles." There is no mention of the *Kent* having been in company, but in his regimental history, Pearse says the two ships parted company off Portsmouth.[34]

In his narrative, MacGregor put a good spin on the passage down Channel.

> The bustle attendant on a departure for India is undoubtedly calculated to subdue the force of those deeply painful sensations to which few men can refuse to yield, in the immediate prospect of a long and distant separation from the land of their fondest and earliest recollections. With my gallant shipmates, indeed, whose elasticity of spirits is remarkably characteristic of the professions to which they belonged, hope appeared greatly to predominate over sadness. Surrounded as they were by every circumstance that could render their voyage propitious, and in the ample enjoyment of every necessary that could contribute either to their health or comfort—their hearts seemed to beat high with contentment and gratitude towards that country which they zealously served, and whose interests they were cheerfully going forth to defend.

Hurried to the westward by "a fine fresh breeze from the northeast," the "stately" *Kent* "speedily passed many a well known spot on the coast, dear to our remembrance." On the evening of

February 23rd, the passengers and crew looked for the last time on "happy England, and entered the wide Atlantic, without the expectation of again seeing land, until we reached the shores of India."[35]

It may indeed have been easier for soldiers and their families who were accustomed to a life of departures and change. All the same, there must have been many with regrets in their hearts, and dread of a voyage where they would be crowded into a ship for three or four months. In their volume of A Picturesque Voyage to India by Way of China, Thomas and William Daniell included a picture of an Indiaman, "Passing Beechy Head," the promontory to the westward of Dover and Folkestone, to which they attached a text:

> Though still in the vicinity of land, the passenger is already liable to the sufferings and dangers of a voyage, and already experiences the hard privations attendant on maritime life. . . The transition from the animated scenes of civilized life, with all its multiplied objects and employments, to the confinement of a ship, is indeed calculated to produce that torpor which should rather be called apathy than rest. Few minds possess sufficient energy to discover in their own reflections a compensation for interrupted habits and pursuits, the suspension of all public and private intelligence, and the absence of all accustomed animation.[36]

The Daniells' description of life onboard an Indiaman is well known:

> The interior of a ship presents society under a phasis equally strange and new. It is not a commonwealth of liberty and equality, but a Chinese system of subordination, with all the minute distinctions of caste, and the watchful jealousy of precedence: it is no community of knowledge; and every individual is restricted to his own department, and interferes not with the duties of another: the steward in the cockpit rarely emerges from his sub-

marine sphere to observe the heavens or the variations of the wind.

Fortunately, the skeletal picture of life on an Indiaman can be fleshed out by the vivid recollections of William Hickey. On his first boarding the *Plassey* at Gravesend at the end of 1768 to begin his first voyage he was agreeably surprised to find that he and two other cadets were to be accommodated in two-thirds of the ship's great cabin. The next day the captain sent word that the "pilot intended to break ground at high water. We accordingly took, as I thought it would be, our last leave of British ground and proceeded to the ship, where we found an excellent dinner just set upon the table, clean, neat, and looking remarkably well cooked, and we were agreeably surprised by being told we should have as good a dinner as we then saw before us every day during our voyage, which certainly was the case." Not all his voyages were so pleasant, however, and when he went out in the *Seahorse* in 1777 he had to share a cabin with three others, and there were twenty-two seated at the captain's table.[37] How all the officers, wives, and private passengers were accommodated at dinner onboard the *Kent* is not known.

T HE day following the *Kent*'s departure from the Downs, February 20th, was a Sunday, and the commander was "strictly required to keep up the worship of Almighty God on board your ship every Sunday, when circumstances will admit, and that the log-book contain the reasons for the omission when it so happens." Without the *Kent*'s logbook, we don't know for certain that service was performed, but regulations were clear on the subject and a very large fine was threatened should any commander fail in this duty:

You are to promote good order and sobriety, by being yourself the example, and enforcing it in others; and that you be humane and attentive to the welfare of those under your command: the Court have resolved to mulct you in the sum of two guineas, for every omission of mentioning the performance of divine service, or assigning satisfactory reasons for the non-performance thereof every Sunday, in the Company's log-book.[38]

The advice given by Mr. Peter Cherry to his daughters in 1821 was that they should not attend divine service on deck unless there was a regular clergyman on board, because "it is too frequent that the person appointed to read the service considered it foreign to his employ and contrary to his inclinations, and you will benefit more by reading the prayers in your cabin."[39] King William's revised charter for the company of 1698 required that a chaplain be carried onboard any ship over 499 tons at the company's expense. As a result, eighteenth-century Indiamen were regularly given fictitious tonnages to spare the cost.[40] That requirement had lapsed by the time *Kent* was built, but concern about the expense has not. There is no indication that there was a chaplain onboard, but if MacGregor read the service, he would certainly have taken his part seriously.

The exact form of religious service used onboard Indiamen is not known, but it might have included the famous Church of England prayer used in the Royal Navy, which begins, "O eternal Lord God, who alone spreadest out the heavens, and rulest the raging of the sea; who hast compassed the waters with bounds until day and night come to an end: be pleased to receive into thy Almighty and most gracious protection the persons of us thy servants, and the fleet in which we serve." Immediately following it in the 1815 Book of Common Prayer was the prayer "to be used in storms at sea," which beings, "O most powerful and glorious Lord God, at whose command the winds blow, and lift up the waves of the sea, and who stillest the rage thereof: We thy creatures, but miserable sinners, do in this our great distress cry unto the for help: Save, Lord, or else we perish."[41]

The presence of women on board could be disturbing, and as a result their life could be quite confined. Cherry was careful to warn his daughters against accepting an invitation to play cards or backgammon, and to be careful of the proprieties should they take exercise on deck. They would be expected to take the arm of a gentleman to ensure they did not fall, but they were to be careful to have a sister on their other arm. Some of the ships brought musicians with them, but the girls were not to dance. Many female passengers were in fact on their way to India to find a husband, and some did indeed find them among those onboard ship. But this was discouraged, and could lead to trouble when rival suitors fought duels. Should a woman find accommodation in one of the officer's cabins, as Mrs. Sherwood did in 1805 when traveling with her husband to India, she would have to retire early into their confined and stinking quarters before the soldiers settled down to sleep on the deck of the steerage.[42]

Apart from divine service, routine called for pumping out the ship's bilges daily, for the officers to "take every favourable opportunity in the course of the voyage, to take lunar observations," and for all the officers and petty officers to keep up their books. Beside the logbook and the medical journal, there was a boatswain's book, a recruit book, a purserage book, and the journals kept by the commander and the first and second mates. The company made its preferences clear:

Such charts as you may receive from this House are to be returned at the end of the voyage with your journals; and the

graduated charts for the ship's track, with variations, longitude
by observation and chronometer, you are particularly directed to
render as complete as possible; and you are to strictly enjoin
your senior officers, and encourage your junior officers, at all
times when practicable, to use the lunar observations, to observe
the variation of the compass by azimuths and amplitudes, finding the latitude by double altitudes, and every other branch of
navigation.[43]

Amplitude tables predicted the degrees of azimuth at which
selected stars appeared above the horizon north or south of due east
or west, so that navigators could check the accuracy of the ship's
compass.[44] Double altitudes is a method for obtaining latitude and
local time from two altitudes of the same celestial body, usually the
sun, usually measured well before and after its transit of the meridian. John Harrison's successful testing in the 1760s of a marine
chronometer that could accurately keep time at sea had made lunar
observations somewhat redundant, but the company requirement
to use the lunar method to determine longitude was an appropriate
precaution against the chronometer being damaged, considering the
very high value of the cargo carried, and the length of the voyages
undertaken by its ships. Observation of the angular distances
between the moon and several fixed stars was intended to obtain an
accurate reading of sidereal time, which could be used to determine
how far east or west they were of the Prime Meridian. But the
mathematics required were extremely difficult. The present location
of the Prime Meridian at Greenwich was not established until 1851,
and did not become internationally recognized until 1884 when
President Chester A. Arthur called an International Meridian
Conference. Nevertheless, British seamen used a line near the Royal
Observatory at Greenwich for their calculations.[45]

In the light of the disaster that later struck the *Kent*, the resolution of the Court of Directors on January 17, 1799, respecting the decorum to be maintained onboard company ships, particularly the use of fire and candles, is most important:

It having come to the knowledge of the Court, that the good order and wholesome practices, formerly observed in the Company's ships, have been laid aside, and late hours and the consequent mischiefs introduced, by which the ship has been endangered, and the decorum and propriety, which should be maintained, destroyed; they have thought proper to frame the following regulations on these points, to which the readiest acquiescence is expected; and any person offending against them will incur the Court's highest displeasure, viz.

Resolved, therefore, that, in order to prevent any accident from the fire and lights being kept up beyond those hours usually observed in all proper disciplined ships, it is strictly enjoined, that no fire be kept up beyond eight at night, unless for the use of the sick, and then only in a stove; and that candles be extinguished by nine between decks, and ten, at latest, in the cabins; and that the utmost precautions be observed, to prevent their being visible to any vessels passing in the night.

That the hour for dinner be not later than two o'clock, and when the commander of the ship retires from table, either after dinner or supper, the passengers and officers of the ship retire also.

While the main concern was the threat of fire, the blackout regulations also reflected a concern about piracy, or sudden attack should war have been declared after the ship cleared land, a distinct possibility in this age.

The requirement for decorum also had other considerations in mind. The commander was "strictly enjoined to pay due attention to the comfortable accommodation and liberal treatment of the passengers, at the same time setting them the example of sobriety and decorum, as he values the pleasure of the Court. . . . Any improper conduct of the officers of the ship towards the passengers or each other, shall be quietly made known to the commander, who shall weigh the circumstances with impartiality, and if conciliation be ineffective, decide according to the best of his judgment, and every person concerned be expected quietly to conform thereto." If anyone persisted in ill-behavior, the commander was to appeal to the governor and council of the first settlement at which the ship touched. But the court recognized that "the diversity of characters and dispositions which must meet on ship-board makes some restraint upon all necessary; and any one offending against good manners, or known usages and customs, will, on representation to the Court, be severely noticed."[46]

How strongly these regulations were enforced may be open to question, but William Hickey's recollections make it abundantly clear that they were very necessary. His experience in the *Seahorse*, under the direction of Captain Arthur, bound for Bengal, is a cautionary tale.[47] Captain Arthur felt himself insulted when some of the passengers did not choose to drink as much wine as he and Hickey thought suitable for a Saturday night. The company quarreled all the way to the Bay of Bengal, and this brought them very close to disaster when one of the passengers, a Colonel Watson, disputed with the captain his astronomical navigation. The fact that the passenger was right only made things worse. In the extensive memoirs Hickey wrote in his retirement he recalled that "Captain Arthur, bursting with rage, looked as red as a turkey cock, puffing and blowing with more than usual violence; but he uttered not a syllable." He refused to let the mates make soundings, and ran on through the night in heavy weather. Finally one of the mates, Mr.

Warre, ordered a hand into the chains ready to take a sounding, and he was

in the act of ordering it, when a man from the bowsprit end cried out "Breakers right ahead and close aboard." In the same moment the leadsman hove the lead; and, finding it directly take the ground, he, in his fright, called out, "There's only three fathom." The utmost confusion and dismay ensued. Captain Arthur ran out of his cabin almost frantic, crying like a child that he was ruined past redemption and had sacrificed his own life, as well as that of all on board. In the most abject and pusillanimous manner he besought the crew and officers to exert themselves, if possible, to save the ship. In his fright he ordered and counter-ordered in the same breath, and was in such consternation he knew not what he said or did.

Mr. Simson [another of the mates], seeing him so incapable, advised his going to his cabin. Mr. Warre had, upon the first alarm, ordered the man at the wheel to put the helm up, braced the yards sharp up, and hauled his wind, heaving the lead as fast as it could be carried forward. The second cast we had ten fathoms, the third only seven, the fourth ten again, then several casts between seven and twelve fathoms; after which it suddenly deepened to twenty-five fathoms, when the risk was supposed to be over; yet so irregular was the bottom that, after having run at least a mile in twenty-five fathom, we had two casts with no more than seven fathom. At daylight, the mainland of Aracan was distinctly seen from deck, with breakers extending a great way out, over which the sea broke with immense fury. Our escape certainly was almost miraculous. Colonel Watson behaved with much moderation and propriety on the occasion; nor did he ever allude to the circumstance afterwards when Captain Arthur was present, a delicacy and forbearance our commander was scarcely deserving of; for his ignorance and obstinate stupidity had nearly cost us our lives.

Captain Cobb commanding the *Kent* was a man of a very different stamp than had been Captain Arthur, 48 years earlier, but it is clear why the Court of Directors felt it important to regulate shipboard life. The officers of the 31st Regiment, and their families, were not given to the sort of high living in which Hickey, the son of a wealthy lawyer, indulged. But perhaps the same sobriety did not extend to all the officers and men of the *Kent*, and perhaps their behavior had a role in the disaster that was to overcome the ship.

Drawings from an American merchantman's log in 1805 showing the effect of heavy weather on a ship at sea. (*Peabody Museum*)

3

The Fatal Spark

BAY OF BISCAY,
FEBRUARY 28–MARCH 1, 1825

ACCORDING TO MACGREGOR'S SURVIVING letter to his father, after dropping the Channel pilot at Land's End at the extreme tip of Cornwall, the *Kent* "continued to proceed for a day or two with a favourable wind." The wind then veered to the southwest and the *Kent* made little progress beating against it. In his narrative, he wrote that the *Kent* encountered some hard winds on the way down Channel and was struck by a "violent gale" from the south west on the night of Monday the 28th at 47°30′ N, 10°00′ W, which gradually increased the following morning.

In 1806, Sir Francis Beaufort, R.N., had begun to use a consistent taxonomy to ensure that terms he used to describe the weather meant the same thing in all his log entries. The following year he developed his concept to make the descriptions more objective, basing his scale on the amount of sail that could be carried on "a well-conditioned man of war." In a "Moderate Gale," for instance, a warship would have its courses double-reefed, but still carry a jib. Progressively, sail area would have to be reduced, in a "Moderate Gale," a "Fresh Gale," a "Strong Gale" and a "Whole Gale." When standing up close-hauled to a whole gale the ship "could only bear close-reefed main top-sail and reefed fore-sail." When she was "reduced to storm staysails" he described the weather as a "storm." Nowhere did he use the term "violent gale."[1] Beaufort's scale, however, did not come into general use until after his appointment as Admiralty Hydrographer in 1829. It was first used by Captain Robert Fitzroy commanding HMS *Beagle* in his 1831 voyage with the naturalist Charles Darwin on board. It was not until 1832 that Beaufort's scale was published, and not until 1838 that the Admiralty ordered it to be employed throughout the Royal Navy.

MacGregor might have been using an earlier scale devised by a Mr. Rous, and published in 1801 by Colonel James Capper of the East India Company.[2] Rous used the term "Violent Storm" to describe winds of 60 knots; and that term was also used in the later revisions of Beaufort's scale. In it the sea condition in a force 11 "Violent Storm" is described as "Exceptionally high waves (small and medium-sized ships might for a long time be lost to view behind the waves). The sea is completely covered with long white patches of foam lying along the direction of the wind. Everywhere the edges of the wave crests are blown into froth. Visibility affected."

Only an artist and critic of the caliber of John Ruskin has the eye and mind to give an adequate description of a storm at sea. In 1848 Ruskin published a book on British painting in which he devoted 55 pages to the problem of painting the sea as part of his study of Joseph Mallard William Turner, the father of English expressionist painting. Turner had had a first-hand experience of a particularly terrible storm at sea, after which he had painted one of his best known canvases with the highly descriptive title of *Snow Storm—Steamboat off a Harbour's Mouth Making Signals in Shallow Water and Going by the Lead. The Author Was in This Storm on the Night the Ariel Left Harwich.*[3] It was a challenging painting for people unused to abstraction, but Ruskin, the best known art critic of the age, considered Turner's *Snow Storm* to be one of his greatest and most truthful paintings:

> Few people, comparatively, have ever seen the effect on the sea of a powerful gale continued without intermission for three or four days and nights, and to those who have not, I believe it must be unimaginable, not from the mere force or size of surge, but from the complete annihilation of the limit between sea and air. The water from its prolonged agitation is beaten, not into mere creaming foam, but into masses of accumulated yeast, which hang in ropes and wreaths from wave to wave, and where one curls over to break forms a festoon like a drapery, from its edge; these are taken up by the wind, not in dissipating dust, but bodily, in writhing, hanging, coiling masses, which make the air white and thick as with snow, only the flakes are a foot or two long; the surges themselves are full of foam in their very bodies, underneath, making them white all through, as the water is under a great cataract; and their masses, being thus half water and half air, are torn to pieces by the wind whenever they rise, and carried away in roaring smoke, which chokes and strangles like actual water. Add to this, that when the air has been exhausted of its moisture by long rain, the spray of the sea is caught by it . . . and covers its surface not merely with the smoke of finely divided water, but with boiling mist; imagine also the low rain-clouds brought down to the very level of the sea, as I have often seen them, whirling and flying in rags and fragments from wave to wave; and finally, conceive the surges themselves

in their utmost pitch of power, velocity, vastness, and madness, lifting themselves in precipices and peaks, furrowed with their whirl of ascent, through all this chaos; and you will understand that there is indeed no distinction left between the sea and air; that no object, nor horizon, nor any landmark or natural evidence of position is left; that the heaven is all spray, and the ocean all cloud, and that you can see no farther in any direction than you could see through a cataract.[4]

A fair estimate is that the *Kent* eventually was subjected to a force 10, "Whole Gale." In the version of his scale that Admiral Beaufort provided for Captain Fitzroy in 1831, force 10 was described as such a wind as a well-found ship of war "could scarcely bear close-reefed main-topsail and reefed fore-sail." Sea conditions in his original official scale for force were described as "Very high waves with overhanging crests; sea takes white appearance as foam is blown in very dense streaks; rolling is heavy and visibility is reduced."

Later, the weather certainly took on that description, but long before that, Captain Cobb had begun to take the canvas off, and ordered the topgallant yards struck down. By ten o'clock on the morning of March 1st, the *Kent* was hove to under a triple-reefed main topsail, with deadlights closed over the windows in the stern gallery. MacGregor says that the weight of hundreds of tons of shot and shells that formed part of the *Kent's* cargo vastly increased the rolling of the ship, which suggests that the first mate, James Sexton, might have been less successful in his stowage than would have been ideal. At about half-past eleven or twelve o'clock, the *Kent* was rolling her main chains under water; and "the best cleated articles of furniture in the cabins and the cuddy were dashed about with so much noise and violence as to excite the liveliest apprehensions of

Snow Storm—Steamboat off a Harbour's Mouth Making Signals in Shallow Water and Going by the Lead. The Author Was in This Storm on the Night the Ariel Left Harwich by J. M. W. Turner, 1842. (*Tate Museum*)

individual danger. The whole watch of soldiers were attached to life-lines that were run along the deck for this purpose." MacGregor busied himself lashing down the furniture in his cabin, and entered into his journal the reading on the marine barometers hanging in the cuddy.

It used to be said that there were no atheists at sea, and certainly MacGregor found that the growing gale affected his thoughts:

> To those who have never "gone down to the sea in ships, and seen the wonders of the Lord in the great deep," or even to such as have never been exposed in a westerly gale to the tremendous swell in the Bay of Biscay, I am sensible that the most sober description of the magnificent spectacle of "watery hills in full succession flowing," would appear sufficiently exaggerated. But

it is impossible, I think, for the inexperienced mariner, however unreflecting he may try to be, to view the effects of the increasing storm, as he feels his solitary vessel reeling to and fro under his feet, without involuntarily raising his thoughts, with a secret confession of helplessness and veneration that he may never before have experienced, towards that mysterious Being, whose power under ordinary circumstances, we may entirely disregard, and whose incessant goodness we are too prone to requite with ingratitude.[5]

In his letter to his father he wrote that "the violence of our rolling was so great that the crew were lashed to the deck, and all our young sailors, and even some of our old ones, looked unusually grave."[6]

In the letter he was to address to his family shortly after returning safely ashore, Dr. Townsend said that "On Tuesday morning it came on to blow a very heavy gale of wind and we were going under a storm staysail and a reefed topsail. I went on deck and never beheld a grander sight than the appearance of the sea running, I may say literally, mountains high; you may form some idea of the waves when that immense ship was rolled about as if it were but a fishing boat."[7] In his first note to his sister he said that the wind was "subsiding" when the heavy rolling and a moment's inattention led to disaster for the *Kent* and her people.

According to the Reverend Rimmell's narrative, "The force of the tempest caused the vessel which contained a heavy cargo, to roll considerably, and rendered it advisable that the third mate, who had charge of the Stores, should examine them in order to discover if any disarrangement of their position had taken place." Muir the third mate found that a cask containing spirits was loose, and ordered a hand to bring some staves to wedge it. "Before he obtained them the ship gave (to use his own words) 'a terrible lounge,' and occasioned the lanthorn to fall from his hand between two casks. In his anxiety to recover the lanthorn he gave up his hold of the loose cask which rolling from its situation, some of the hoops the violent action of the ship had loosened, dropped off, the spirit escaped, and coming into contact with the flame of the candle ignited and the hold was speedily in a blaze."[8] Muir tried for some minutes to contain the fire himself, but then sent to inform Captain Cobb "about seven o'clock."

Why there was a cask of spirits in the hold was not explained; it might have been part of the cargo. The main supply of potable spirits were further aft in the spirit room.

The best account of what happened was taken down as evidence by Colonel Fearon soon after the event. The first witness was Sergeant John Jack of the regiment, who stated that he had heard a noise coming from the casks which sounded as though they had got loose. "His wife heard it also, but knowing it could only be one of the casks, that had fetched way, he took no farther notice."

[Jack] was lying on the Larboard side of the Orlop deck with his family, when about 12 o'clock the 3rd Mate [Mr. Muir] came to the after hatchway, and after unlocking the grating descended into the hold with two other men. In a short time he return'd and gave the lamp to be trimmed, and after receiving it back, he again went down into the hold, and a few moments after he called out in a most impatient manner to bring him some wood; upon which a bundle of staves, (being a cask that had been emptied, broken up and hooped together with the iron hoops that lay near) was handed to him; shortly after he ejaculated "D—n the fellow, he has dropt the lamp between the rum casks;" and returning called for some water, when a bucket was immediately handed to him, and either one or more subsequently, but he added, when calling for the water "D—n you! Don't make a noise to alarm the ship." He [Sergeant Jack] then ran to the hold mouth, and the flame burst forth instantaneously upon him from the rum casks stowed amidships forward, as far as he could guess from the second cask.[9]

Another witness was Mary Healy, daughter of private Charles Healy who was one of those who did not survive the disaster. She was employed as a maid servant by the colonel's wife, Mrs. Fearon, but seasickness had driven her to the orlop, where she was lying in a swinging cot near the entrance to the hold, looked after by her mother. Her account was virtually identical to Sergeant Jack's. MacGregor thought it was the mate who had dropped the lantern, but evidently that was not the case.

It is possible that the noises Sergeant Jack and his wife had thought was simply the result of a cask working loose was in fact the sound of someone seeking "liquid courage" in the gale and trying to broach the barrel. The company's concern about "decorum" on the part of crew and passengers was specifically connected with the fear of fire and fear that insobriety could lead to carelessness. The fact that the hold grating was locked does not preclude this possibility, because someone might have obtained a copy of the key. But at any rate, on the basis of the evidence he had collected, Colonel Fearon later felt able to assure the commander-in-chief that none of the soldiers had been the cause of the fire.[10]

Suddenly the scene was transformed. MacGregor remembers that he had just satisfied the request of "one of the women" onboard that he read to her "the 12th chapter of St. Luke, which so beautifully declares and illustrates the minute and tender Providence of God, and so solemnly urges on all the necessity of continual watchfulness and readiness for the 'coming of the Son of Man'":

Fear him, which after he hath killed hath power to cast into hell;
yea, I say unto you, Fear him. Are not five sparrows sold for two
farthings, and not one of them is forgotten before God? But even
the very hairs of your head are all numbered. Fear not therefore:
ye are of more value than many sparrows. Also I say unto you,
Whosoever shall confess me before men, him shall the Son of
man also confess before the angels of God.[11]

In his letter to his father, MacGregor said that he had just left
Elizabeth and Joanna "when an officer as pale as death met me, and
wringing his hands, said: 'Sir, the ship is on fire in the after hold!'"
In his narrative he described the scene more dramatically, saying
that Captain James Spence of the 31st, who was the regimental captain of the day, burst into the great cabin with the terrible information that the ship was on fire. MacGregor rushed to the hatch
where he found Captain Cobb already directing the fire fighting,
using the pumps, buckets, and soaked sails and hammocks. He
decided he should take word to Colonel Fearon, "and, not to alarm
his family, I called him out, and in a whisper told him our awful
condition." In his narrative he said he reassured the ladies that
there was no immediate danger, as the burning cask was surround-
ed by water casks. Very soon, however, this confidence was found
to be mistaken, when the light blue vapor from the burning spirit
was succeeded by a thick black "dingy" smoke which poured up
from all four hatches, and indicated that the fire had ignited the hay
stowed to feed the cows that were onboard to provide milk, and
had reached the cable tier where the tarred hemp anchor cable was
flaked down.

The immediate casualties were among the soldiers and their families sleeping in the orlop and gun decks. When Dr. Townsend ran
up on deck dressed only in his trousers he found them struggling up

the ladders from below. Not all of them made it into the fresh air. Those soldiers on the sick list, a woman whom Captain Spence identifies as Mrs. Molloy, and her three children, were killed by the smoke.[12] Captain Bray says that 11 children died from the smoke.[13] Muir, who was himself almost overcome, stumbled over their bodies. "The horror that was not observable baffles all my powers of description," MacGregor told his father. "Elizabeth and Joanna were comparatively composed, but the screams of some of the other ladies and of the soldiers' wives who came running from the lower decks . . . was piercing. . . . Our driblets of water poured down from the buckets were absolutely useless. Wet sails, blankets, and other woollen articles were thrown down in the hope of their smothering the flames, but all to no purpose." The Reverend Rimmell tells us that the soldiers and women who had been in their beds enduring seasickness, "rushed upon deck, and gave utterance to their feelings in cries; which, blended with the roaring of the winds, the agitation of the waters, and the prevalence of the smoke, that partially obscured the atmosphere, produced an effect the most awful; a scene which none can ever wish to behold, and which those who witnessed will never forget."[14]

"Imagine to yourself the horror of our situation," Captain Bray later recalled. "A single ship at sea 200 miles from shore, no vessel in sight. Death appeared inevitable. Everyone now used their utmost efforts to preserve the ship, some drew up buckets of water, others cut holes in the deck to let it run down." But more drastic measures were required. "In these awful circumstances," MacGregor wrote in his narrative, "Captain Cobb, with an ability and decision of character that seemed to increase with the imminence of the danger, resorted to the only alternative now left him, of ordering the lower decks to be scuttled, the coamings of the hatches to be cut, and the lower ports to be opened, for the free admission of the waves." MacGregor went below with Colonel Fearon, Captain Bray, and several other officers to carry out the orders, and there encountered Muir "staggering towards the hatchway, in an exhausted and nearly senseless state."

> So dense and oppressive was the smoke, that it was with the utmost difficulty we could remain long enough below to fulfill Captain Cobb's wishes; which were no sooner accomplished, than the sea rushed in with extraordinary force, carrying away, in its resistless progress to the hold, the largest chests, bulkheads, &c. Such a sight, under any other conceivable circumstances, was well calculated to have filled us with horror; but in our natural solicitude to avoid the more immediate peril of explosion, we endeavoured to cheer each other, as we stood up to our knees in water, with a faint hope that by these violent means we might be speedily restored to safety.[15]

MacGregor later reflected that the high sea and the ship's heavy rolling, which had contributed so greatly to the circumstances leading to the disaster, had also made it possible to contain the fire, because of the speed with which the water flooded in when the ports were opened. But the water did not quench the fire altogether, and the ports had to be shut again if the ship were not to sink:

> The immense quantity of water that was thus introduced into the hold had indeed the effect, for a time, of checking the fury of the flames; but the danger of sinking having increased as the risk of explosion was diminished, the ship became water-logged, and presented other indications of settling, previous to her going down. Death, in two of its most awful forms, now encompassed us, and we seemed left to choose the terrible alternative.[16]

In his account of the disaster, Charles Dickens remarked that "there were a few lives to be sacrificed in order that many might be saved. The axes went to work, the timbers crashed in, over them and through them lept the water, immediately drowning several sick soldiers, poor women, and shrieking children, whose cries were, however, in a moment stilled."[17] But anyone remaining below deck had undoubtedly already died from the smoke, and the axes if used were only to knock out the wedges keeping the hinged ports tightly closed, and possibly to cut through the hatch coamings on deck.

Cobb then tried to suffocate the fire: "always preferring the more remote, though equally certain crisis, we tried to shut the ports again, to close the hatches, and to exclude the external air, in order, if possible, to prolong our existence, the near and certain termination of which appeared inevitable." But closing down all the ports and hatches was found to be inadequate to quench the fire, and Cobb ordered that a hole be cut in the foredeck to create a draft that would draw the fire away from the spirit room in the after hold. As the powder magazine was forward of the fire, this was a desperate measure, but it was hoped that the water casks between the cable tier and the magazine would stop the fires advance before it reached the powder kegs. Had the *Kent* been built in the traditional manner, with an open waist amidships, it would not have been possible to have controlled the draft in this way.

The awful realization that there was little or no chance of living through the night was now all too clear to the passengers and crew crowding the upper decks. The Biscay storm still raged, and some who had gone miserably to their bunks with seasickness had stumbled up the ladders in panic without even clothes to protect them from the weather. Families had become separated and were desperately looking for each other. MacGregor says that their reactions to their fate ranged from "silent resignation," or "stupid insensibility" to the "most frantic despair." For some, the instinct was to their religion. "Some on their knees were earnestly imploring, with significant gesticulation, and in noisy supplications, the mercy of Him, whose arm, they exclaimed, was at length outstretched to smite them; others were to be seen hastily crossing themselves, and performing the various external acts required by their peculiar persuasion."

> Several of the soldiers' wives and children, who had fled for temporary shelter into the after-cabins on the upper decks, were engaged in prayer and in reading the Scriptures with the ladies, some of whom were enabled, with wonderful self-possession, to offer to others those spiritual consolations which a firm and intelligent trust in the Redeemer of the world appeared at this awful hour to impart to their own breast. The dignified deportment of two young ladies, in particular, formed a specimen of natural strength of mind, finely modified by Christian feeling, that failed not to attract the notice and admiration of every one who had an opportunity of witnessing it.[18]

Captain Spence identified the two ladies as Joanna Dick and Elizabeth Fearon, the colonel's eldest daughter Margaret-Eliza, and when the narrative was reprinted a year later, MacGregor or the editor added to his account, saying that,

> On the melancholy announcement being made to them, that all hope must be relinquished, and that death was rapidly and inevitably approaching, one of the ladies above referred to, calmly sinking down on her knees, and clasping her hands together, said, "Even so come, Lord Jesus," and immediately proposed to read a portion of the Scriptures to those around her; her sister, with nearly equal composure and collectedness of

mind, selected the forty-sixth and other appropriate Psalms, which were accordingly read, with intervals of prayer, by those ladies alternately, to the assembled females.[19]

"God *is* our refuge and strength," Psalm 46 begins, "a very present help in trouble. Therefore will not we fear, though the earth be removed, and though the mountains be carried into the midst of the sea; *Though* the waters thereof roar *and* be troubled, *though* the mountains shake wih the swelling thereof."

With less of a flourish, and with more conviction, MacGregor's account to his father was that

> some were now filled with terrible despair—others were very properly imploring the mercy of that God who alone could pardon and save us. Elizabeth and Joanna were the organs of prayer to as many females as could find access to their cabin. It is quite impossible for a human being to be nearer to death without tasting it, than we were, and believed ourselves to be at that tremendous hour.
>
> Notwithstanding that those whom I most loved were about to share with myself the same melancholy fate, I declare that I really felt as great a composure and collectedness of mind, as I do at this moment. I felt the nearness of my Redeemer. . . . I look back with utter amazement at the strength that was given me. . . . Elizabeth and myself had determined to sink in each other's arms. She was wonderfully composed, but Joanna's conduct was magnanimous in the highest degree.[20]

The scene must have been very similar to that shown in the aquatint engraved by "E. W." of the last moments of the Indiaman *Halswell* which sank in 1786 (see frontispiece). MacGregor's choice of words make this display of piety ring untrue, and perhaps he was embroidering the truth to serve his evangelical purpose. But mental habits, carefully developed, do provide the spiritual armor needed in time of crisis, as much by soldiers and their families, as by the general public. Death is the business of soldiers, and a major concern of the evangelical:

> One young gentleman, of whose promising talents and piety I dare not now make further mention, having calmly asked me my opinion respecting the state of the ship, I told him that I thought we should be prepared to sleep that night in eternity; and I shall never forget the peculiar fervour with which he replied, as he pressed my hand in his, "My heart is filled with the peace of God;" adding, "yet, though I know it is foolish, I dread exceedingly the last struggle."
>
> Amongst the numerous objects that struck my observation at this period, I was much affected with the appearance and conduct of some of the dear children, who, quite unconscious in the cuddy-cabins, of the perils that surrounded them, continued to play as usual with their little toys in bed, or to put the most innocent and unseasonable questions to those around them. To some of the older children [Colonel Fearon's children], who seemed fully alive to the reality of the danger, I whispered, "Now is the time to put in practice the instructions you used to receive at the Regimental School, and to think of that Savior of whom you have heard so much." They replied, as the tears ran down their cheeks, "O Sir, we are trying to remember them, and we are praying to God."[21]

In contrast to this piety was the stoicism of some of the "older and more stout-hearted soldiers and sailors" who "sullenly took their seats directly over the magazine, hoping, as they stated, that by means of the explosion which they every instant expected, a speedier termination might thereby be put to their sufferings." And MacGregor did not find a great deal of "true" religion among the apparently doomed men. "The passive condition to which we were all reduced, by the total failure of our most strenuous exertions, while it was well calculated, and probably designed, to convince us afterwards, that our deliverance was effected, not 'by our own might or power, but by the Spirit of the Lord,' afforded us ample room at the moment for deep and awful reflection, which, it is to be earnestly wished, may have been improved, as well by those who were eventually saved, as by those who perished." But not many appeared to put their remaining hours to such good use. "If I were to judge of the feelings of all on board, by those of the number who were heard to express them, I should apprehend that a large major-ity of those men, whose previous attention has never been fairly and fully directed to the great subject of religion, approach the gates of death, it may be, with solemnity, or with terror, but without any definable or tangible conviction of the fact, that 'after death cometh the judgment.'"

> Several there were, indeed, who vowed in loud and piteous cries, that if the Lord God would spare their lives, they would thence-forward dedicate all their powers to his service; and not a few were heard to exclaim, in the bitterness of remorse, that the judgments of the Most High were justly poured out upon them, for their neglected Sabbaths, and their profligate or profane lives; but the number of those was extremely small, who appeared to dwell either with lively hope or dread on the view of an opening eternity.22

A young man who had been introduced to MacGregor sometime before the voyage, apparently by an evangelical friend, later confessed "that though he was at that moment fully persuaded of the certainty of immediate death, yet the subject of eternity, in any form, had not once flashed upon his mind, previously to my conversation." It seems that they both climbed the mizzen shrouds at the same time, and had discussed such things in what was practically speaking an elevated situation.

For some, religion was manifested in superstition. MacGregor writes that while the passengers and crew

> lay in a state of physical inertion, but with all our mental faculties in rapid and painful activity—with the waves lashing furiously against the side of our devoted ship, as if in anger with the hostile element for not more speedily performing its office of destruction—the binnacle, by one of those many lurches which were driving every thing moveable from side to side of the vessel, was suddenly wrenched from its fastenings, and all the apparatus of the compass dashed to pieces upon the deck; on which, one of the young mates, emphatically regarding it for a moment, cried out with the emotion so natural to a sailor under such circumstances, "What! Is the *Kent*'s compass really gone?" leaving the bystanders to form, from that omen, their own conclusions. Lieutenant Booth, a "promising young officer of the troops, was seen thoughtfully removing from his writing-case a lock of hair, which he composedly deposited in his bosom.[23]

MacGregor himself wrote a last pious letter to his father, which he corked up in a bottle. "I never saw anything like the coolness of Major MacGregor," Townsend later described to his family. At the time when "we were quite certain of perishing, he got some paper, wrote the name of the vessel, put it in a bottle, and had only to throw [it] overboard, in order to inform our friends what had become of us, preventing any vain hopes of seeing us again."[24]

"The ship the *Kent* Indiaman is on fire—Elizabeth, Joanna, and myself, commit our spirits into the hands of our blessed Redeemer; his grace enables us to be quite composed in the awful prospect of entering eternity D. M'GREGOR 1st March 1825 Bay of Biscay."[25]

The note that Duncan MacGregor sealed in a bottle and threw overboard when he assumed his family would perish aboard the *Kent*. The bottle washed ashore in Barbados a year and a half later and the note was recovered. (*from the 1885 edition of MacGregor's narrative*)

A Brig in a Sea with a Distant Coast by James Chrisholme Gooden. This painting is a good representation of a ship of *Cambria*'s type. (*NMM PAD8991*)

4

Cambria

LTHOUGH DESPERATE, THE MEASURES THAT Captain Cobb had taken served to buy time, containing the fire amid-ships for eleven hours, so that it did not reach either the spirit room aft nor the powder magazine forward, and did not even burn through the tiller ropes. The time this gained for the passengers and crew was priceless. No vessel had been sighted for several days. According to her log, the *Scaleby Castle* estimated her position on February 28th, at 49°0′8″ N, 10°17′ W. No lunar sight had been attempted, perhaps because of the heavy weather, but if the *Scaleby Castle*'s reckoning, and MacGregor's statement about the *Kent*'s position, were accurate, they would have been about 100 miles apart.[1] There could be no help from that quarter, but in the lull after the frantic activity below fighting the fire, the fourth mate, John Thomson, sent a man aloft on the foremast. It must have been a hideous climb with the ship rolling as she was, but when he got to the top and looked around the horizon everything was in an instant changed. The watchers on deck saw him reach the top and raise his head to scan the sea, "a moment of unutterable suspense," and then they saw him wave his hat and hail that he had seen "a sail on the lee bow!" Suddenly the apathy of despair gave way to hope that eternity might be deferred.

The cheers with which this was greeted may well be imagined. The *Kent's* topsails and fore sail were braced round to put her as near as possible on a course to close with the ship beating to windward, flags were hoisted upside down as a signal of distress, and signal guns were fired. It was doubtful whether the guns could be heard because of the gale. It was even possible that the ship, or rather brig, which turned out to be the *Cambria*, would ignore the signals. The *Cambria* was such a small vessel that, according to one of her passengers, when both ships were in the send of the sea, the *Kent* was completely hidden to sight by the towering waves in between. But the black smoke pouring from the hole in the *Kent's* foredeck was a clear indication of the peril, and the *Cambria's* captain, William Cook, was not one to ignore mariners in distress. After ten or fifteen minutes, the anxious watchers on *Kent's* deck saw British colors run up, and the *Cambria* crowd on sail to close the distance as rapidly as possible.

Captain Bray wrote that "a faint ray of hope began to animate every bosom. It was a faint one, the ship was barely in sight and it would take a long time to come to us, if she came at all—we hoisted a signal of distress and fired minute guns—the stranger approached, saw our signal and bore up for us."[2]

The *Cambria* was one-seventh the size of the *Kent*, a brig of about 200 tons that had been built in 1816, in Swansea, Glamorganshire in Wales. When she was re-registered under new ownership in London on January 12, 1825, William Cook was named both as commander and as his own managing owner, with

32 of the 64 shares. Cook was an Ayrshire man then living at King Street, Finsbury in the County of Middlesex.[3] The remaining 32 shares were divided between William Birch, merchant, and John Hare "the younger," floor cloth manufacturer, both residing in Bristol. The survey officer, James Mason, described the *Cambria* as having two decks, two masts, a length of 84 feet 6 inches, and a breadth above the wales of 24 feet. She was square rigged with a standing bowsprit, a square stern, no stern galleries, and carvel planking. Below deck the headroom was only 5 feet 2 inches.[4]

"IT is a singular fact," commented the Reverend Rimmell, "that Captain Cook witnessed the building, the launching, and the destruction of the *Kent*."[5] Cook was almost certainly on his first voyage as owner and commander of the *Cambria* when he played a central part in the *Kent's* last act. His charter was to Vera Cruz, Mexico, carrying 26 Cornish tin miners and Yorkshire smelterers who had been recruited by the Anglo–Mexican Association; several agents of the firm were also onboard.

It was the wars of liberation throughout the Spanish empire, and the opportunity this gave to British financial interests to become partners in the metal mines of the New World, that brought the Cornish miners that stormy day to the middle of the Bay of Biscay. Tin had been mined in Cornwall since the Bronze Age, about 2150 B.C., and the Cornish mines were still flourishing in the early nineteenth century. With tunnels stretching under the sea, Cornwall led the world in the introduction of steam pumps. It was because of their great experience that the miners had been recruited by the newly formed Anglo–Mexican Association, and they were to exert a disproportionate influence modernizing Mexican and South

American mines, making possible the development of modern global mining corporations.[6]

The German engineer and traveler Alexander von Humbolt had visited the fabulous Veta Madre silver mine at Mina Valenciana in 1799, and had published an account of it in 1811. That same year the first steam engine was introduced into a Latin American mine, an engine built by Richard Trevithick, a Cornishman, that was shipped to Peru and carried by mules up the Andes. When production at Mexican mines ceased because of the fighting that led in 1821 to the declaration of the "Mexican Empire," and the revolution in 1823 that created the United Mexican States, London financial circles saw their opportunity. The British Real del Monte Company had been formed in London in 1824, with managers and technicians leaving England on March 25, 1824. Soon after, the Anglo–Mexican Association had been established with offices at 7 St. Helen's Place, Bishopsgate, in the City of London, and had commenced work at Guanajuato, Mexico, in August 1824.[7] A total of 44 new mining companies were registered in London during this period, and 50 percent of them were interested in Latin America.[8]

A letter posted by one of the first immigrants, Captain Thomas Garby, Jr. to J. T. Tregelles of St. Agnes in Cornwall, September 18, 1824, was printed in the *Royal Cornwall Gazette* in January 1825: "You may suppose that after a residence of upwards of a month I should be prepared to give you some description of the place, with an idea of our future prospects, but it would baffle a much brighter genius than mine to give you an adequate description of it. I can only say that in a landscape it is more romantic than I, or I believe few Englishmen, could imagine."[9] According to the *Gazette*, the town of Falmouth in Cornwall was transformed by the mining boom, its streets "thronged with people—the hotels and principal houses consequently filled—as the agents and others engaged for

the different mining speculations
abroad are assembled and waiting to
sail for their various destinations."[10]

On Wednesday November 24,
1824, the Secretary of the Anglo–
Mexican Association, Joseph Lowe,
had advertised in the *Times* that it
was intended to charter a ship of
300–350 tons at Swansea, and
another of 150–250 tons on the
Thames, for passage to the Gulf of
Mexico.[11] The *Cambria* had been
built at Swansea, but it was as a
London ship that she was selected.
MacGregor tells that the *Cambria*
had been detained in Falmouth nearly a month, and when finally she was
clear of the land Cook laid off the

A miniature portrait of Captain
William Cook of the *Cambria*
painted by C.F. Thatcher, presumably after Cook's return to
London following the rescue of
the *Kent* survivors. (*Mary
Wallace*)

same course as the *Kent*, but a long way ahead of her. According to
Captain Cook's later report to the ships agents at Lloyd's insurance,
William Broad and Sons, the *Cambria* sailed on February 24th
from Falmouth.

Had all gone well, the *Cambria* would never have known about
the *Kent's* distress. However, the *Cambria* was unable to hold her
course for the Atlantic crossing because of the force of the wester-
ly gale. A heavy sea broke over her quarter and damaged her bulwarks on the windward side allowing the breaking seas to pour
across the deck, and Cook was obliged to put her on the other tack
to keep the water out, putting her on a course which brought her
into sight of the *Kent*. On March 1st, Cook wrote, he had the
Cambria hove to "under a close-reefed main topsail" in 47°30′N,

9°45′W, when a large sail was seen to the westward. Probably as a result of Captain Cobb's bringing the *Kent* before the wind to close with the *Cambria*, her distress signals were seen. Disregarding the damage to his ship's side, Cook immediately squared up to windward to close the distance, and it was at that point that the smoke from the fire was seen.

Having reached a position close to leeward of the *Kent* but not so close as to be in danger from the fire, Cook again hove the *Cambria* to, ready to receive survivors. In order to do so, he must have had the fore topsail, and possibly the fore topmast staysail, drawing to balance the main topsail. To bring her as nearly as possible to a stop, her reefed main and fore topsails would have been braced hard on the wind in a close-hauled trim. The fore topsail would have been braced round aback with the two weather yard arms of the main and fore topsails almost touching. The helm would have been put hard-a-lee, and her small forward motion would have served to keep her up into the wind. If the fore topmast staysail was also backed, it would have been necessary to avoid putting too much strain on the masts, as the standing rigging would have been set up with an after bias. Too much strain on the fore stays could have dismasted her.[12]

In his letter to his father, MacGregor wrote that, as the fire had been burning for some hours and the sea so "tremendously high— and as no small vessel and few large ones could be expected in addition to their own crew, to take on board nearly 700 human beings—neither Captain Cobb, Colonel Fearon, nor myself entertained much hope."[13] In his narrative he wrote that "it was impossible, and would have been improper to repress the rising hopes that were pretty generally diffused amongst us by the unexpected sight of the *Cambria*, yet I confess, that when I reflected on the long period our ship had been already burning—on the tremendous sea that was running—on the extreme smallness of the brig, and the immense number of human beings to be saved, I could only venture to hope that a few might be spared; but I durst not for a moment contemplate the possibility of my own preservation." Nonetheless, there was hope, and much would depend on the discipline of crew and passengers if any were to escape.

The *Kent*'s boats had been hoisted on board for the long voyage to India, and secured along the ship's side. In his narrative MacGregor painted a picture of good shipboard discipline, enforced by the officers. He wrote that Captain Cobb gave the order to lower the first of the boats, the cutter, when the *Cambria* was leeward of the *Kent*'s bow. One of the officers asked in what order the men should move out, and MacGregor recorded that he had answered, "Of course in funeral order." Colonel Fearon immediately confirmed that "Most undoubtedly the juniors first," and then added the order, "see that any man is cut down who presumes to enter the boats before the means of escape are presented to the women and children. . . . To prevent the rush to the boats, as they were being lowered, which, from certain symptoms of impatience manifested both by soldiers and sailors, there was reason to fear, some of the military officers were stationed over them with drawn swords. But from the firm determination which these exhibited, and the great subordination observed, with few exceptions, by the troops, this proper precaution was afterwards rendered unnecessary."14

Reverend Rimmell is a little more frank, writing that when orders were given to get out the boats, "some of the crew, uninfluenced by those humane feeling which generally characterise British seamen, manifested a disposition to cut them down and provide for their own safety at the expense of their companions in distress; nor did they desist from the attempt until several of the military officers

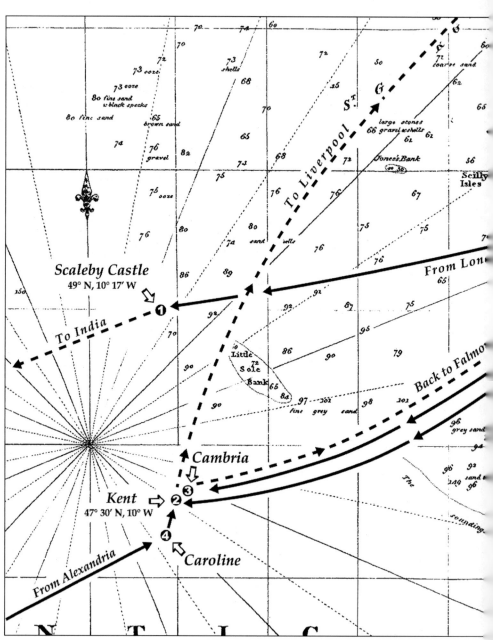

Detail from the Admiralty's 1825 "General Chart of the Coasts, from the River Thames and locations of *Scaleby Castle* (1), *Kent* (2), *Cambria* (3), and *Caroline* (4) on March 1, 1825.

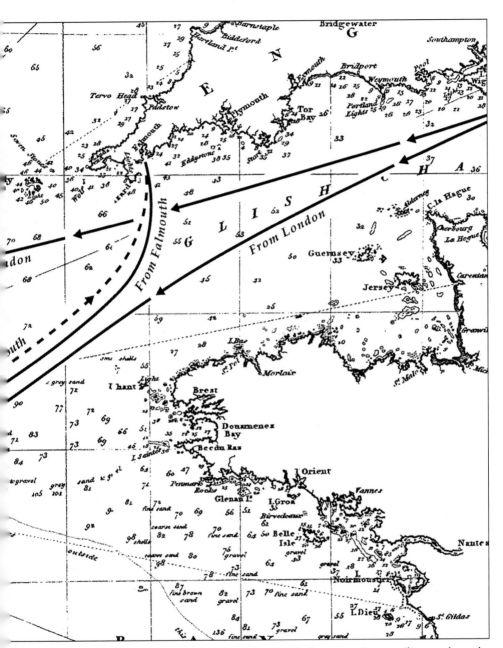

the South Part of Ireland to the Mediterranean Sea," with the approximate sailing tracks and

drew their swords and threatened to kill the first man who should act contrary to orders."[15]

But in his letter to his father, MacGregor revealed the full extent of the panic, and how it was met. In the midst of the howling gale, with towering seas, a fire onboard, and explosion expected at any moment, some of the men were overcome by their fears and selfishness, and paid an awful price in consequence. "Seeing that some of the sailors were preparing to cut away our boats with a view to provide for their own safety only, Colonel Fearon, myself, and two other officers, stationed ourselves conveniently with our drawn swords to cut down the first man who should touch the boats without orders, or dare to enter them until the means of escape had been presented to the poor women. It was impossible notwithstanding, to prevent a rush into the first boat that was launched, which was in consequence instantly swamped, and the work of death was begun. The miserable men on board of it we saw struggle for moment with the breakers, and then disappear forever."

Townsend thought this episode happened later in the day, but supplies the information that it had been the gig, the smallest of the ship's boats, that was rushed and swamped.[16]

To prevent a repetition of that panicked rush, Captain Cobb decided to load the officers' wives and as many of the soldiers' wives as possible into the cutter before it was lowered, strict "funeral order" not being applied to the women and children. As the cutter was hanging over the quarter, Cobb ordered that the women should climb into it through the cuddy window. "My dearest lassie," MacGregor wrote, "implored for leave to remain with me, but on reasoning with her calmly for a moment she consented to proceed. At this instant shall I attempt to describe my agony of mind?"[17]

In his narrative, MacGregor states that it was about 2:30 when they mustered outside the after cabins dressed in whatever warm

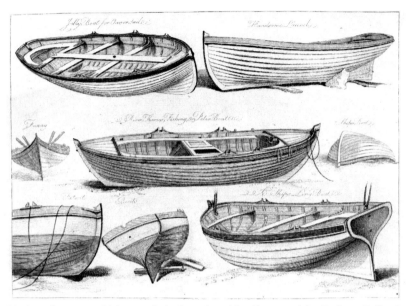

Various boats could be carried aboard a ship. Engraved by Robert Pollard, they are from left to right, top to bottom: a jolly boat, a handsome launch, tunny, River Thames fishing or Peter boat, ships boat, patent boats, and a ship's long boat. The cutter was similar to the long boat, and the gig, the *Kent*'s smallest boat that was swamped, was similar to the tunny. (*NMM PAD7749*)

clothes they could find. "Scarcely a word was uttered—not a scream was heard—even the infants ceased to cry, as if conscious of the unspoken and unspeakable anguish that was at that instant rending the hearts of their parting parents—nor was the silence of voices in any way broken, except in one or two cases, where the ladies plaintively entreated permission to be left behind with their husbands."[18] There was no time to waste, and they "successively suffered themselves to be torn from the tender embrace. . . . With the fortitude which never fails to characterize and adorn their sex on occasions of overwhelming trial, were placed, without a murmur, in the boat, which was immediately lowered into a sea so tempestuous as to leave us only 'to hope against hope,' that it should live in it for a single moment." MacGregor "stood outside on the chains to lift them into the boat." He had thrust forty or fifty gold sovereigns into his pocket handkerchief, and gave them to his wife before she clambered into the cutter to be ferried to the *Cambria* so that she would have provision for herself should he not make it out of the *Kent*, and she should find herself alone in a foreign country.

John Thomson, the fourth mate, was put in command of the cutter. The seamanship required for heavy weather boat work is of the highest order. For the *Kent* to get her boats into the water was itself a highly demanding task in a heavy sea. The falls rigged to the fore and aft ends of the boat had to be checked away at the same speed and unhooked just as the boat reached the water. Later in the century several "quick release" gears were developed that made it possible for one man to disconnect simultaneously both ends of the boat from the falls, but none was available in 1825, and safety depended on the bowman and coxswain working perfectly together. If a boat should be detached from one of the falls only it would be dragged nearly vertically by the other in the next send of the sea, throwing everyone into the water where they would certainly drown. MacGregor writes that this fate was only narrowly averted.

> Although Captain Cobb had used every precaution to diminish the danger of the boat's descent, and for this purpose stationed a man with an axe to cut away the tackle from either extremity, should the slightest difficulty occur in unhooking it; yet the peril attending the whole operation, which can only be adequately estimated by nautical men, had very nearly proved fatal to its numerous inmates.
>
> After one or two unsuccessful attempts to place the little frail bark fairly upon the surface of the water, the command was at

length given to unhook; the tackle at the stern was, in consequence, immediately cleared; but the ropes at the bow having got foul, the sailor there found it impossible to obey the order. In vain was the axe applied to the entangled tackle. The moment was inconceivably critical, as the boat, which necessarily followed the motion of the ship, was gradually rising out of the water, and must in another instant have been hanging perpendicularly by the bow, and its helpless passengers launched into the deep, had not a most providential wave suddenly struck and lifted up the stern, so as to enable the seamen to disengage the tackle; and the boat being dexterously cleared from the ship, was seen, after a little while, from the poop, battling with the billows; now raised, in its progress to the brig, like a speck on their summit, and then disappearing for several seconds, as if engulfed "in the horrid vale" between them.[19]

In his letter, Townsend said that the cutter had been caught up on the chains "and half filled with water." But it is unclear whether that was subsequent to the problem clearing the falls, or was how that crisis looked to him.

In his own letter to his father, MacGregor admitted that when he handed in his infant "and saw the boat lowering down into an ocean so tempestuous that no sailor on board thought it would live for a moment, I grew blind. But my confidence was in the Lord my God. Twice the cry was that the boat was swamped. It at last was seen fairly clear of the ship, and encountering the billows. Sometimes it disappeared for several seconds."[20]

The boat seems to have been on the leeward quarter of the *Kent*, but there would nevertheless have been a real risk of it being stove in against her side if the crew were not able to get her away quickly. For that reason a "boat-rope" could have been rove from the bow of the boat to a forward position in the *Kent* so that her forward motion could be used to enable the crew to use the rudder to sheer off from the side. Once clear, the boat-rope had to be cast off quickly before it caught the bow around and brought the boat crashing back into the ship's side. In the *Admiralty Manual of Seamanship*, coxswains are warned: "You must get clear of the ship the moment your boat is slipped, so while the boat is being lowered warn your crew to stand by to bear off hard from the ship's side immediately when she is slipped. If the boat-rope is made fast in the boat ensure beforehand that it can be slipped easily, and give the order to slip it before the boat sheers too far out from the ship's side." The recommended method of securing the boat-rope so that it could be slipped quickly was to lead the eye on its end under the forward thwart of the boat and hook it with a small timber laid across that and the thwart next aft. All that was then needed to cast off was to jerk the timber clear of the loop on the boat-rope.[21]

Once away, the boat's crew had to work their way to the *Cambria* through the mountainous sea of a Biscay gale. The 1908 *Admiralty Manual of Seamanship* did not mince words in describing the dangers of running to leeward before a broken sea. Although written with the dangers of landing on a beach in mind, the advice given also applies to open ocean boat work: "The one great danger, when running before a broken sea, is that of broaching-to. To this peculiar effect of the sea, so frequently destructive of human life, the utmost attention must be directed." If the boat is in effect surfing on the leading edge of a wave its stern will rise, and its bow be driven into the trough. The resistance forward will cause the stern to swing parallel to the sea, or even cause it to pitch-pole over the bow. In either case the boat will be overturned and the men thrown into the sea; "in this way many lives are annually lost amongst merchant seamen." The only way to prevent this from happening is to slow the boat as the waves pass under it, backing water with the oars, or using a drogue (sea anchor).

MacGregor tells us that:

> The *Cambria* having prudently lain to at some distance from the *Kent*, lest she should be involved in her explosion, or exposed to the fire from our guns, which, being all shotted, afterwards went off as the flames successively reached them, the men had a considerable way to row; and the success of this first experiment seeming to be the measure of our future hopes, the movements of this precious boat in calculably precious, without doubt, to the agonized hus-

"Saved from the Wreck," an engraving from the 1885 edition of MacGregor's narrative, shows the *Kent*'s cutter bringing the first passengers to the *Cambria*.

> bands and fathers immediately connected with it were watched with intense anxiety by all on board. The better to balance the boat in the raging sea through which it had to pass, and to enable the seamen to ply their oars, the women and children were stowed promiscuously under the seats, and, consequently, exposed to the risk of being drowned by the continual dashing of the spray over their heads, which so filled the boat during their passage, that before their arrival at the brig, the poor females were sitting up to the breast in water, and their children kept with the greatest difficulty above it.[22]

The Admiralty advised that:

A ship should almost always be boarded on her lee side, and the best position is where her freeboard is lowest and as near amidships as possible, where the vessel's pitching and yawing will be least felt. . . . On no account should an attempt be made to board a ship's weather side, because the seas will fling the boat against it and probably smash or swamp her. If the ship is lying beam on to the sea there will probably be a considerable swirl and backwash round her bows and stern; and if lying with the sea on her bow and pitching, there will probably be a considerable swirl and undertow at her bows and especially at her stern: a boat should therefore always give a wide berth to the bows and stern of a vessel hove to. . . . The vessel being boarded should provide fenders lowered to the waterline, a jumping ladder and lifeline, and a long boat-rope which should have a long eye spliced in its end and be led well forward so as to allow the boat to rise and fall on the waves independently of the ship. While the boat is alongside a hand should be stationed in her bows to slip or cut the boat-rope immediately should the need arise.

But the *Cambria* was lying to leeward of the wreck—in the direction the wind and waves were moving—because it would be easier for survivors to reach her in that position, and it appears from MacGregor's account that the *Kent*'s fourth mate, John Thomson, came alongside the *Cambria*'s windward side about 3:00 p.m. in clear view to the men on the *Kent*'s upper deck:

In the course of twenty minutes, or half an hour, the little cutter was seen alongside "the ark of refuge;" and the first human being that happened to be admitted out of the vast assemblage that ultimately found shelter there, was the infant son of Major

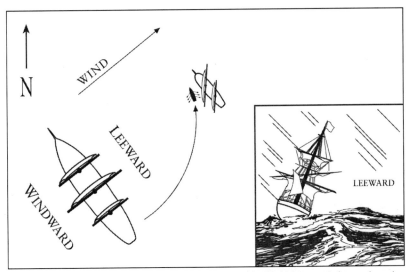

The *Cambria* (right) hoved to on the leeward side of the *Kent* (left) so that the boats could make a quicker passage to the brig. The *Kent*'s cutter apparently approached the *Cambria* on its windward side despite the danger of collision, perhaps because the mate felt that the leeward side of the *Cambria* (inset) could be driven violently down on the cutter due to the storm or that the cutter might be trapped below *Cambria*'s chains plates on that lower side.

Macgregor, a child of only a few weeks, who was caught from his mother's arms, and lifted into the brig by Mr Thomson.

But the extreme difficulty and danger presented to the women and children in getting into the *Cambria* seemed scarcely less imminent than that which they had previously encountered; for, to prevent the boat from swamping, or being stove against the side of the brig, while its passengers were embarking from it, required no ordinary exercise of skill and perseverance on the part of the sailors, nor of self-possession and effort on that of the females themselves.[23]

It was Thomson's responsibility to make the decision how he would approach the *Cambria*, and, despite the Admiralty recommendation to avoid the weather side, it is recognized that it may occasionally be safer for a boat to approach the windward side of a ship that is hove to in a gale. Because of her greater windage, there was a danger that the ship would drive so rapidly down on the boat coming alongside to leeward, pushing it violently against the water, that it would be in great danger of capsizing and throwing its people into the water. Another consideration was that the *Cambria*'s rope shrouds would have been kept taut by lanyards rove through dead eyes led outboard of the bulwarks to the channels, and then to the chains at her beam ends. Hove to, the channels and chains on the *Cambria*'s leeward side would have been low to the water because of the 10 to 20 degree list caused by the wind in her sails. Thomson may have seen that there was a danger of the cutter being trapped beneath them, and opted for the windward side where the windward channels would be well clear of the water.[24] There would still have been a very real danger of the cutter being stove in by beating against the side of the brig, and getting the people up the higher windward side would have been more difficult, but the *Cambria*'s slow forward motion would have been enough to make use of a boat-rope effective for holding the cutter off. And the passengers were to find that help getting on board was at hand.

Captain Cook ordered the children be brought onboard first, followed by their mothers, who had to leap from the thwarts (the oarsmen's seats across the boat) hoping to grasp the hands of those leaning over to help. If they were to miss their aim, they would certainly fall into the sea and have been drowned or crushed between the ship's side and the boat. Fortunately, none did, except for one who missed the reaching hands, but succeeded in grasping a rope hanging over the ship's side. She clung there, and was eventually dragged on board. The Cornish miners and Yorkshire smelterers

The Loss of the Indiaman Kent by Joseph William Wildey, painted around 1825. The enormous seas encountered throughout the rescue operation are clearly portrayed. (*The Royal Museum & Art Gallery, Canterbury*)

had climbed over the brig's gunwale onto the rigging channels where they could reach the exhausted people when the seas tossed up their boat, and swing them onboard. This was dangerous work requiring the great strength they had. Many survivors arriving with little or no clothing were supplied with the miners' and the agents' own clothing and bedding.

The Rimmell narrative describes the scene:

When the cutter reached *Cambria*, the females clad only in their night garments, were in a state of extreme debility; but (and we consider it a providential occurrence) there were in the Brig individuals whose hearts as the seat of benevolent feeling, contained a richer treasure than the mines they were proceeding to explore; though like the precious ore which they search for and refine, it may be concealed by a rough exterior. . . . One and all exerted themselves to get the ladies on board, which was a work of considerable difficulty. Several of the strongest of them took their station in the chains of the vessel, and availing themselves of the short interval which elapsed between the return of successive waves, seized the feeble sufferers and delivered them into the arms of their "comrades" who were upon the deck. In this employment [James] Warren and Karkeek, two eminent Cornish wrestlers, were particularly distinguished, they acted as if sensible they could not employ the muscular energy with which Heaven had favoured them to greater advantage, and they had the pleasure of witnessing their combined efforts crowned with success.[25]

One woman, who Captain James Spence tells us was Mrs. Kuff, arrived in the advanced stages of pregnancy, and was to give birth two hours after being pulled onboard the *Cambria*. Unfortunately, James Warren was to pay a heavy price for his efforts. His health was seriously affected and he was later judged by a doctor in Falmouth to need extended bed rest.[26]

"I have reason to know," MacGregor wrote, "that the feelings of oppressive delight gratitude, and praise, experienced by the married officers and soldiers, on being assured of the comparative safety of their wives and children, so entirely abstracted their minds from their own situation as to render them for a little while afterwards totally insensible either to the storm that beat upon them, or to the active and gathering volcano that threatened every instant to explode under their feet."

Having successfully discharged the first boat load of women and children, the *Kent*'s cutter crew panicked when Mr. Thomson

One of the several paintings by Thomas Buttersworth of the destruction of the Indiaman *Kent* on March 1–2, 1825. The time depicted is after the flames broke out of the hold and brought down the masts, but before the explosion of the powder magazine. The cutter used to bring the survivors to the *Cambria*, is shown continuing its rescue operations, which it did until about midnight. (*Courtesy of Mary Wallace, photograph by Stuart Green*)

ordered them to let go of the *Cambria* and return to the *Kent* for a second cohort. They had good reason for their fears. The gale was unabated, and the danger to the cutter and her crew of working her back to windward to the *Kent* was scarcely less than it had been running to leeward. "As a general rule," the Admiralty advised, "speed must be given to a boat rowing against a heavy surf. Indeed, under some circumstances, her safety will depend on the greatest possible speed being attained on meeting a sea. . . . The great danger is that an approaching heavy sea may carry the boat away on its front, and turn it broadside-on, or up-end it, either effect being immediately fatal. A boat's only chance in such a case is to obtain sufficient way to enable her to pass, end on, through the crest of the sea, and leave it behind her as soon as possible." The seamen at the oars had to drive the boat as hard as they could to give her enough speed and inertia to enable her to resist the force of the waves, and fourth mate Thomson had to do what he could to avoid the breaking crests. If the oarsmen were able to give the cutter more speed than was needed to prevent her being carried back by a surf, Thomson might be able to ease the passage through the top of the wave by checking them on its approach.[27] It all required the greatest degree of experience, and brutal labor.

Cook reported to Lloyd's his "great disappointment with the conduct of the cutter's crew (in which I am borne out by Captain Cobb,) derogatory in every respect to the generally received character of a British seaman, by refusing to return to the *Kent* for the people after the first trip." The voice of authority had to be raised in the strongest way: "my utmost exertions and determination" was needed "to compel them to renew their endeavours to get out the soldiers, passengers, and the remainder of their own shipmates who were left behind." It was only by using "coercive measures, in conjunction with my own crew and passengers, and telling them I would not receive them on board unless they did so, that they proceeded though reluctantly, in their duty." Thomson and Mr. Philips the boatswain were made of sterner material, and Cook bestowed on them his "warmest praise."

In his letter to his father, MacGregor said that the boat's crew "sought refuge in the rigging" but that the Cornish miners "seized the poltroons by the neck and heels, and threatened to throw them into the water if they did not return to our assistance."[28] The correspondent for the *Times* wrote that "had the *Cambria* not had the miners on board, it is a query if one-half of the people would have been rescued." "The crew of the *Cambria* and the miners lined the side, and by force prevented . . . [the *Kent* cutter crew] coming into the vessel, until they had gone back and made further exertions to save their fellow creatures."[29] A later account suggests that Cook was concerned that the *Kent*'s sailiors might seize the *Cambria* and abandon the rescue operation.[30] Once their first and baser instincts had been checked, however, the seamen of the *Kent* returned to their work and plied their oars in the mountainous seas until long into the night. Townsend was to tell his sister that Thomson made six return trips to the *Kent*: "He is a very young man and deserves the greatest praise."[31]

Thomas Butterworth's dramatic *The Loss of the East Indiaman Kent in the Bay of Biscay, 1 March 1825*. This is perhaps the most accurate illustration of the rescue effort. (*NMM BHC3819*)

5

Courage, Faith, and Fire

BAY OF BISCAY, MARCH 1–2, 1825

WHEN THE *KENT*'S CUTTER EVENTUALLY PULLED BACK to the hulk, the spreading of the fire, and the danger from the guns "cooking off," discharging violently through the closed gun ports, made it necessary for Thomson to find a way of taking people onboard over the stern, despite the backwash and the way the *Kent* may have been making, but this maneuver confused those on board. In his letter, MacGregor said that the cutter "lay off too far to let the men get into it, and in despair the soldiers tried to find some powder to fire into them to bring them to." But he made no mention of that in his narrative, perhaps after having had a chance to talk to Thomson about the reason for the delay.

The first idea was to lower people down on a rope, two at a time. A start was made with two of the women who had not found a place in the cutter on her first crossing. This proved a very difficult

operation because the heaving of the ship made it all but impossible to time the descent so that the people were put into the boat
rather than dunked into the sea. No woman was drowned in this
operation, but all were repeatedly submerged in the sea. The children fared far worse, and parents watched with horror as several of
the younger were drowned. In desperation several soldiers leaped
into the water to rescue their children, and were themselves
drowned.

MacGregor wrote that "one young lady, who had resolutely
refused to quit her father, whose sense of duty kept him at his post,
was near falling a sacrifice to her filial devotion." This was none
other than Margaret-Eliza Fearon. Townsend, in his letter, writes
that she "was six times under water before she was taken in, and
had the presence of mind enough to hold the rope tied round her
waist, so to keep herself uppermost." It is probable that her sense
of duty was to the other women of the regiment, as well as to her
father. She was taking the role of the Colonel's wife, because the
present Mrs. Fearon had young children for whom her responsibil-
ities were immediate. Once she had shown the way, "all the soldier's wives were then got up on the poop" to be lowered in the
same way into the boats.[1] But it was to take hours before the last
of them was transferred.

"Another individual," MacGregor wrote, "who was reduced to
the frightful alternative of losing his wife or his children, hastily
decided in favour of his duty to the former. His wife was accordingly saved, but his four children, alas! were left to perish." And the
catalogue of woe continued:

A fine fellow, a soldier, who had neither wife nor child of his
own, but who evinced the greatest solicitude for the safety of
those of others, insisted on having three children lashed to him,

with whom he plunged into the water. Not being able to reach the boat, he was again drawn into the ship with his charge, but not before two of the children had expired. One man fell down the hatchway into the flames, and another had his back so completely broken as to have been observed quite doubled falling over-board. These numerous spectacles of individual loss and suffering were not confined to the entrance upon the perilous voyage between the two ships. One man, who fell between the boat and the brig, had his head literally crushed to pieces; and some others were lost in their attempts to ascend the sides of the *Cambria*.[2]

Richard Cannon's regimental history of the 31st fills in the tragic detail of the story of Sergeant Jack, his wife and his family, the soldier whose testimony about the first moments of the fire was recorded by the Colonel:

> Among the children lost there were four, three girls and a boy, the family of Serjeant Jack, an old and deserving soldier, who had seen much service with the second battalion in the Peninsula. While the women and children were being lowered into the boats, Mrs. Jack fell overboard; the serjeant leaped into the sea to save his wife, and was not able to return to the ship. In the confusion unavoidable on board, the children were overlooked; missing their parents, they had sought refuge, it is supposed, in the Colonel's cabin, and no one knew, until it was too late, that they were still on board; for the soldiers were not backward in giving their aid to save the families of their comrades.[3]

MacGregor states that when all of the *Kent*'s boats and those from the *Cambria* were launched, there was a total of six boats working back and forth between the two ships. But Captain Cook told the Lloyd's agent that he had refused the offer of the leaders of the Anglo–Mexican Association, Lucas and Parker, and of the miners, to take a place on the rowing benches. This he said he had "good reason to prevent." It may be supposed that every Cornishman, even if a miner, had some experience at sea, but Cook wanted only professionals in the sea condition then prevailing. MacGregor tells us that in the course of the day, three of the six boats "were either completely stove in, from being thrown against the sides of the ships, or were swamped." And when they were, the speed with which some of the men disappeared beneath the towering waves was believed to have been caused by the weight of the "spoils" they had helped themselves to in the cabins.

The Rimmell narrative states that "of six boats which were in employ during the afternoon, only three remained at night, and one of these had an hole in its bottom which was stuffed up with soldiers jackets." In his letter Townsend particularized that it was the launch that was kept afloat by stuffing a soldier's blanket into its damaged bow. Townsend also noted that, "The only sailor who perished was present in the hold at the time or very shortly after the commencement of the fire, when, availing himself of the confusion which followed its discovery, he hastened to the cabin of the second mate, forced open the desk, and took from thence four hundred Sovereigns, which he rolled up in an handkerchief and tied round his waist; but in attempting to leap into one of boats, it is supposed he fell short and the weight of his spoils caused him immediately to sink."[4]

The process of transferring the women and children was taking so long that it was decided that any soldiers who could get themselves onboard one of the boats, without slowing the painstaking business of lowering the women, should do so. This led to several precipitantly throwing themselves into the sea, where they promptly sank. "One poor fellow of this number, a very respectable man,

Just in Time by Thomas Hemy. Note the spanker boom and the person being lowered by a rope from atop the stern.

had actually reached the boat, and was raising his hand to lay hold on the gunnel, when the bow of the boat, by a sudden pitch, struck him on the head, and he instantly went down."[5] This was the husband of the woman who had stowed away at Gravesend, and then again at Deal. To nineteenth-century readers, this grim spectacle naturally brought to mind the lines from William Falconer's *The Shipwreck*, Canto 2, 356–363:

> *Prone on the midnight surge with panting breath*
> *They cry for aid, and long contend with death;*
> *High o'er their heads the rolling billows sweep,*
> *And down they sink in everlasting sleep.*
> *Bereft of power to help, their comrades see*
> *The wretched victims die beneath the lee;*
> *With fruitless sorrow their lost state bemoan,*
> *Perhaps a fatal prelude to their own!*

If anything that happened on the *Kent* can be said to be humorous, it was the sudden change of heart by one of the sailors who had seated himself on the hatch over the powder magazine, hoping that his death would be quick when the fire reached the kegs. As the time passed, and many of his fellows were seen to be successfully reaching the *Cambria*, he pretended to be disappointed, and exclaimed: "Well! if she won't blow up, I'll see if I can't get away from her." He found his way into one of the boats and MacGregor believed that he reached safety.

All the same, the fire was visibly burning forward toward the powder magazine. Colonel Fearon and Captain Cobb decided that something had to be done to speed up the debarkation. The stern remained the only place where this could be done. It was decided to suspend a rope from the end of the spanker boom which projected over the stern rail, so that the men could work their way along the boom and climb down the rope well clear of the ship. This proved to be an improvement, but it had its own difficulties. MacGregor tells us that "from the great swell of the sea, and the constant heaving of the ship, it was impossible for the boats to preserve their station for a moment." The result was that those who succeeded in making their way to the end of the boom, which was in itself a very difficult undertaking for landsmen in any circumstances, but much more so with the ship rolling and pitching as she was, and then succeeded in climbing down the rope, it was likely that they would have to hang onto the end for some time before they could be pulled into a boat. "Those who adopted this course incurred so great a risk of swinging for some time in the air, and of being repeatedly plunged under the water, or dashed against the sides of the boats underneath, that many of the landsmen continued to throw themselves out of the stern windows on the upper deck, preferring what appeared to me the more precarious chance of reaching the boats by swimming."[6]

A lithograph by Joseph Martin Kronheim, *Loss of the Kent East Indiaman*, showing the rescue operation. The illustration is inaccurate in its rather calm portrayal of the gale force conditions at the time. (*NMM PAD6401*)

This is the scene which was later painted by William Daniell, showing the boat laying to a painter, and people clambering along the spanker boom to let themselves down clear of the rudder. The rate at which people could be transferred from the hulk was agonizingly slow, and the emotional strain enormous. A lithograph of the same subject, but with a deceptively calm appearance, was later published by Joseph Martin Kronheim.[7]

The transfer was taking so long, and the danger of explosion getting ever greater, that Captain Cobb ordered rafts made from spars, hen coops, and other available material in the hope that they could provide a means of getting people off the ship and into the boats. They did not prove effective for that purpose because, no sooner were they put over the side, than they were dashed to pieces. Later, their wreckage would provide a precarious refuge for some of the men. Everyone was ordered to tie a rope around his or her waist so that they could be used to secure them to a raft if need be. MacGregor was amused by one soldier who felt he needed to ask permission before helping himself to the rope securing an officer's cot; but he was moved by the fortitude displayed by the soldiers in meeting their fate.

Having evacuated most of the women and children, and many of the rank and file, the officers began to take their place in the queue of men waiting to crawl along the spanker boom, and clamber down the rope suspended over the raging sea. He noticed that their discipline was rigid and their courage convincing, none betraying an "unmanly or unsoldier-like impatience to quit the ship." He also noticed that none made a parade of their courage in order to hide an underlying timidity. Each took his place in a boat with his soldiers. He particularly commented on the conduct of Colonel Fearon who provided effective leadership throughout the day despite his concern for his family. Orders were calmly given, and were obeyed with "promptitude and respect."

MacGregor felt that the 31st Regiment had earned the approval of His Royal Highness, the Commander-in-Chief. As an indication of the strength of the regimental feeling, MacGregor tells that when some of the soldiers found a box of oranges they did not take any until they had offered a share to their officers. But he admits that it was not just the officers and men of the 31st who behaved well; so did the cadets of the East India Company's army, and even the private passengers.

Perhaps recognizing that this account was not entirely true of all onboard, MacGregor went on to discuss just how the people he observed dealt with their fear. He says he would have expected to have seen a whole spectrum of reactions ranging from the evident courage and "decided heroism" of some down to "the lowest degree of pusillanimity and frenzy discoverable in others."

However, what he actually saw was that there was a broad line dividing the majority who were "greatly elevated by the excitement above their ordinary standard," and "the incalculably smaller, but more conspicuous group, whose powers of acting and thinking became absolutely paralysed, or were driven into delirium, by the unusual character and pressure of the danger." Even more interesting was that some who were rendered incapable by fear later got a grip on themselves "by some great internal effort," and showed their underlying courage. And others found their courage "suddenly giving way, without any fresh cause of despair." He suggested that these anomalies might be easily accounted for, but in reality his observations were sophisticated for his time.

MacGregor's account of his own reactions are no less interesting:

Some of the soldiers near me having casually remarked that the sun was setting, I looked round, and never can I forget the intensity with which I regarded his declining rays. I had previously felt deeply impressed with the conviction, that that night the ocean was to be my bed; and had, I imagined, sufficiently realized to my mind both the last struggles and the consequences of death. But as I continued solemnly watching the departing beams of the sun, the thought that that was really the very last I should ever behold it gradually expanded into reflections, the most tremendous in their import. It was not, I am persuaded, either the retrospect of a most unprofitable life, or the direct fear of death or of judgment, that occupied my mind at the period I allude to; but a broad, illimitable view of eternity itself altogether abstracted from the misery or felicity that flows through it,— a sort of painless, pleasureless, sleepless eternity. I know not whither the overwhelming thought would have hurried me, had I not speedily seized, as with the grasp of death, on some of those sweet promises of the gospel, which give to an immortal existence its only charms, and that naturally enough led back my thoughts, by means of the brilliant object before me, to the contemplation of that "blessed city, which hath no need of the sun, neither of the moon to shine in it; for the glory of God doth lighten it, and the Lamb is the light thereof."

"I have been the more particular in recording my precise feelings at the period in question," he continued, "because they tend to confirm an opinion which I have long entertained." People of MacGregor's background and religious persuasion were, he wrote, "in the habit of uttering the awful words, Almighty, heaven, hell, eternity, divine justice, holiness, without attaching to them, in all their magnitude, the ideas of which such words are the symbols. How much is it to be lamented, that we do not keep in mind a truth which no one can pretend to dispute, that our indifference or blindness to danger, whether it be temporal or eternal, cannot possibly remove or diminish the extent of it."[8]

The scene changed with the coming of night. The increasing cold drove MacGregor into the cuddy to find a blanket, and there he found physical and spiritual desolation. This had been a cheerful place where the passengers gathered. Now it was deserted by all but a few who had slaked their fear with spirits and had become so intoxicated that they had fallen to the deck, and a few others who were "prowling about like beasts of prey in search of plunder." Apparently, there was plenty for them to pocket, because the officers of the 31st Regiment, who might at any time have come below to collect their belongings, had refrained from doing so "to avoid even the appearance of selfishness, at moments when the valuable lives of their sailors and soldiers were at stake." They did not want to take any time for their own private concerns when their men also faced disaster and could not get below to find their belongings

William Daniell, *The Loss of the Kent Indiaman*, aquatint published in 1825. The review of this painting by Timothy Flint and Washington Irving in *The Knickerbocker* noted that Daniell chose for his subject the time about three hours after the fire was ignited. "The *Cambria* is seen bearing down from the distance to save the sufferers—some of whom are represented as clinging to the shrouds and rigging, and others hurrying from the terrific fire, which gleams wildly upon the raging element below—upon a boat crowded with affrighted passengers, and just about to be swallowed up by the hungry surge—and upon the agonized features of those who, having failed to reach the craft, are struggling with the billows as they roll over them. The whole picture is a powerful embodiment of the saying, that "Fire and Water are good servants, but hard masters." (*NMM 8440*)

because of the fire on the lower decks. The senior officers with cabins on the upper deck had most to lose, but apparently had the self-discipline to let it go. The furniture was scattered and broken, first by the violent rolling of the ship, and then by the violence of the looters. Among the ruins were geese and a solitary pig that had escaped their pens in the forecastle.

Oppressed by the scene and bothered by the smoke which came through the deck, MacGregor returned to the poop where he found the few officers that remained: Captain Cobb, Colonel Fearon, Lieutenants Ruxton, Booth, and Evans, superintending the disembarkation. Most of the sailors seemed to have found a way of leaving the ship, and the soldiers who remained found light-colored towels to wrap around their heads so that they would be easier to see in the now-dark water.

After each boat load left, those men remaining had approximately 45 minutes to wait for its return, and MacGregor employed the time in asking his companions about their feelings. Some of them "after remaining perhaps for a while in silent abstraction, would suddenly burst forth, as if awakened from some terrible dream to a still more frightful reality, into a long train of loud and desponding lamentation, that gradually subsided into its former stillness." It was during those trying intervals when the boats were away that religious instruction and consolation appeared to MacGregor to be the most required, and the most acceptable. His object was a religious one, to help his companions prepare for the prospect of death, but it was also practical. When writing his narrative he asked the less religiously minded readers to consider how important it was for the survival of the men to address their fears so that they could in their turn crawl the length of the spanker boom, now in a dark only broken by the smoky glow of the fire below decks, and then climb down the rope toward the sea. The habit of military discipline had become tenuous for these exhausted men; only religion answered their fears, and at that only the religion of Grace.

> I well remember that no arguments tended to soothe their troubled minds but those which went directly to assure them of the freeness and fullness of that grace which is not refused, even in the eleventh hour, to the very chief of sinners.

And if any of those to whom I now allude, have been spared to read this record of their feelings in the prospect of death, it will be well for them to keep solemnly in mind the vows they then took upon them, and to seek to improve that season of probation which they so earnestly besought, and which has been so mercifully extended to them, by humbly and incessantly applying for accessions of that faith which they are sensible removed the terrors of their awakened consciences, and can alone enable them henceforward to live in a sober, righteous, and godly manner, and thereby give the only unquestionable proof of their love to God, and their interest in the great salvation of his Son Jesus Christ.[9]

With the return of each boat, another cohort made the trip over the stern to safety. "I must state, that in general it was not those most remarkable for their fortitude who evinced either a precipitancy to depart, or a desire to remain very long behind—the older and cooler soldiers appearing to possess too much regard for their officers, as well as for their individual credit, to take their hasty departure at a very early period of the day, and too much wisdom and resolution to hesitate to the very last." But among the remaining men there were some who found they did not have the resolution, or the ability, to leave. Captain Cobb was forced again and again to urge the men to be quick, and MacGregor said that one of the officers, one who had expressed his intent to stay to the last man, reinforced the appeals with a threat to wait no longer. Some of the men begged to be lowered over the stern in the same way the women had been, but this was not allowed, and the three remaining officers prepared for their own departure. With two boats astern ready to receive men, all who could or would make the attempt could be accommodated. The wreck, which was already nine or ten feet below the ordinary water-mark, had sunk two feet lower since the last trip and there was no time to be wasted.

In his letter to his father, MacGregor wrote that Colonel Fearon, "who could not be of any further use on board the *Kent*, and might be of some service in the brig in hastening the boats, attempted to escape by dropping from the boom in question, by a swinging rope, in doing which he was so frequently dashed against the side of the boat below, and by the heaving of the ship plunged so deeply into the water, that all thought he was gone. He was however preserved, but with one leg so bruised as to require the greatest care to prevent the most serious consequences." He only survived because someone grabbed his hair as he was submerging, and pulled him onboard.

Townsend's own escape was similar:

About half past six in the evening Colonel Fearon (who behaved nobly) went into one of the boats and then Mr. Baldwin (a court-ly gentleman who behaved as well as possible, a fine fellow) and I thought it time to try and get off. We went out to the end of the spanker boom which was no very easy job; several times I thought I should have been thrown off from the lurchings of the vessel. However, I held on and got hold of a rope that was hang-ing from the end and when the boat came under with a wave, we dropped into it. I had neither shoes nor stockings and lost all my property. However, I can never feel sufficiently grateful to Almighty Providence for having preserved me from the most horrible of deaths. It was very dangerous approaching the brig [the *Cambria*] and getting out of the boat; many soldiers were drowned in [the act of] getting out, one poor fellow who was in the boat with me when getting up was struck by the boat and had his thigh broken to pieces. Another poor fellow earlier in the day was struck on the head [by the boat, which crushed it] . . . as if it were an eggshell. God grant that I may never witness such a scene again. A sailor who went down the rope I escaped by, missed the rope and went to the bottom. I saw him go under; he never rose again.[10]

MacGregor remained for some time because he had pledged himself to the soldiers' wives that he would not leave himself until all of them were safely off the ship. "The presence of a few of them still in the burning ship, kept me and two other officers on board for an hour after the time I now allude to." One of the soldiers, "a noble little kind fellow, who was particularly active in saving the women, having received a terrible blow in the chest, I ordered on the boom, as I saw him still disposed to remain. I then directed our excellent serjeant-major to proceed, and, having seen the last woman fairly off, the officers and myself prepared to depart."[11]

As I cannot perhaps convey to you so correct an idea of the condition of others, as by describing my own feelings and situation under the same circumstances, I shall make no apology for detailing the manner of my individual escape, which will sufficiently mark that of many hundreds that preceded it.

The spanker boom of so large a ship as the Kent, which projects, I should think, 16 or 18 feet over the stern, rests on ordinary occasions about 19 or 20 feet above the water; but in the position in which we were placed, from the great height of the sea, and consequent pitching of the ship, it was frequently lifted to a height of not less than 30 or 40 feet from the surface.

To reach the rope, therefore, that hung from its extremity, was an operation that seemed to require the aid of as much dexterity of hand as steadiness of head. For it was not only the nervousness of creeping along the boom itself, or the extreme difficulty of afterwards seizing on, and sliding down by the rope, that we had to dread, and that had occasioned the loss of some valuable

lives, by deterring the men from adopting this mode of escape;
but as the boat, which the one moment was probably close under
the boom, might be carried the next, by the force of the waves,
15 or 20 yards away from it, the unhappy individual, whose best
calculations were thus defeated, was generally left swinging for
sometime in mid-air, if he was not repeatedly plunged several
feet under water, or dashed with dangerous violence against the
sides of the returning boat; or, what not unfrequently happened,
was forced to let go his hold of the rope altogether.

As there seemed, however, no alternative, I did not hesitate,
notwithstanding my comparative inexperience and awkward-
ness in such a situation, to throw my leg across the perilous
stick; and with a heart extremely grateful that such means of
deliverance, dangerous as they appeared, were still extended to
me; and more grateful still that I had been enabled, in common
with others, to discharge my honest duty to my sovereign and to
my fellow soldiers; I proceeded, after confidently committing my
spirit, the great object of my solicitude, into the keeping of Him
who had formed and redeemed it, to creep slowly forward, feeling at every step the increasing difficulty of it. On getting nearly
to the end of the boom, the young officer whom I followed, and
myself, were met with a squall of wind and rain, so violent as to
make us fain to embrace closely the slippery stick, without
attempting for some minutes to make any progress, and to excite
our apprehension that we must relinquish all hope of reaching
the rope. But our fears were disappointed; and after resting for
a while at the boom end, while my companion was descending
to the boat, which he did not find until he had been plunged
once or twice over head in the water, I prepared to follow; and
instead of lowering myself, as many had imprudently done, at
the moment when the boat was inclining towards us, and consequently being unable to descend the whole distance before it

William Daniell, *The Cambria Brig, Receiving on Board the Last Boat Load From the Kent East Indiaman on Fire*, aquatint, 1826, from a painting commissioned by Stewart Marjoribanks, owner of a majority of shares in the *Kent*, exhibited at the Royal Academy in 1826. (*NMM 4573*)

again receded, I calculated that while the boat was retiring I ought to commence my descent, which would probably be completed by the time the returning wave brought it underneath; by which means I was, I believe, the only officer or soldier who reached the boat without being either severely bruised or immersed in the water.[12]

MacGregor helped pull an oar, and then faced the dangers of getting onboard the *Cambria*, assisted "by a friendly hand which pulled me, with a heart oppressed with joy and praise, into the ark of refuge."

For the women and children waiting to learn the fate of their husbands and fathers, it had been a dreadful time. MacGregor recalled:

I cannot pretend to give you any adequate idea of the feelings of hope or despair that alternately flowed like a tide in the breasts of the unhappy females on board the brig, during the many hours of torturing suspense in which several of them were unavoidably held respecting the fate of their husbands; feelings which were inconceivably excited, rather than soothed, by the idle and erroneous rumors occasionally conveyed to them regarding the state of the *Kent*. But still less can I attempt to portray the alternate pictures of awful joy and of wild distraction exhibited by the sufferers, (for both parties for the moment seemed equally to suffer,) as the terrible truth was communicated, that they and their children were indeed left husbandless and fatherless; or as the objects from whom they had feared they were for ever severed, suddenly rushed into their arms.[13]

To his father MacGregor would be more explicit:

It seems that the agony of mind evinced by Elizabeth, the darling, during the many long hours she had for reflection on my account, on board the brig, was painful to all around her. As boat after boat arrived, with officers and passengers, her piteous inquiries for me were heartrending. Her cousin, David Pringle, on his arrival endeavoured to prepare her for the worst. But she says her hopes did not entirely die within her until the arrival of Colonel Fearon, who, from his manner more than his words, expressed but little hope. What greatly increased her horror was, that the arrival of each boat being announced, her spirits were buoyed up for a moment, and then to be broken, as the loud gratulation was given to the officers who successively arrived! At last however the Lord, who never tempts above that which we are able to bear, turned my darling's mourning into great gladness—the news of my arrival was scarcely conveyed to the cabin, when I had her and my dearest Joanna in my arms. Poor dear lassie—she was stupefied—my cup ran over—we could not speak—but God knows our hearts were fulled with the praises of the Lord.[14]

John MacGregor's biographer adds the family tradition that when Colonel Fearon came on board the *Cambria* Joanna tried to speak to him but he went straight to the cabin where Duncan's wife was; and there his first words were, "I Fear poor MacGregor is gone!"

That he proved wrong was a blessing to Elizabeth and her family, but MacGregor writes that their joy was, "speedily chastened, and the attention of all arrested, by the last tremendous spectacle of destruction."[15] Townsend told his sister that he "watched the wreck from the stern window, about 9 o'clock she was enveloped in flames and about 2 in the morning blew up, it was the grandest and most awful sight I ever witnessed and when I reflected what a short time had elapsed since I left her, I could not help feeling—but words cannot convey my feelings."[16]

"The Magazine Exploded," from the 1885 edition of MacGregor's narrative.

6

Abandoned

BAY OF BISCAY, MARCH 2, 1825

ITH THE COMING OF THE NIGHT, the time was fast approaching when the *Cambria* would have to abandon her rescue operation. For those now crammed into her decks, it was becoming a matter of the greatest urgency to get them to shore where their needs could be met. Onboard the *Kent*, even Captain Cobb had come to realize he could do nothing more for the remaining men who were unable to find the resolution or ability to make their ways into one of the boats. MacGregor writes that Captain Cobb "finding all his entreaties fruitless, and hearing the guns, whose tackle was burst asunder by the advancing flames, successively exploding in the hold into which they had fallen . . . at last felt it right to provide for his own safety, by laying hold on the topping-lift or rope that connects the driver boom with the mizentop, and thereby getting over the heads of the infatuated men who occupied the boom, unable to go either backward or forward, and ultimately dropping himself into the water."[1]

When questioned by the War Office as to why anyone had been left onboard, Captain Cook told them the information he had received from the officers commanding the boats, that they "could not prevail on the unfortunate men to leave the ship, many of them being in a state of intoxication." Captain Cobb, "who was amongst the last to quit the *Kent*," confirmed that report. When the last boat that returned from the *Kent* brought only one person in it, and the ship was completely enveloped in flames, he could not ask his men to make another attempt. "I, however, kept the men in the boats about two hours, that in case of the explosion taking place we might endeavour to save some from the wreck. After this period I took the men out of the boats and made sail, thinking it impossible to render any further assistance to the unfortunate people left on board and who I judged by this time must have perished." In his own defense, he added his belief that if the *Kent*'s crew had used "proper exertion," and been assisted effectively by the soldiers, everyone might have been saved.[2]

MacGregor also reported that the *Cambria* had done everything it could to save every man.

One of the boats persevered in keeping its station under the *Kent*'s stern, not only after all expostulation and entreaty with those on board had failed, but until the flames, bursting forth from the cabin windows, rendered it impossible to remain, without inflicting the greatest cruelty upon the individuals that manned it. But even on the return of the boat in question to the *Cambria*, with the single soldier who availed himself of it, did Captain Cook, with characteristic jealousy, refuse to allow it to come alongside, until he learned that it was commanded by the spirited young officer, Mr Thomson whose indefatigable exertions, during the whole day, were to him a sufficient proof that all had been done that could be done for the deliverance of those individuals.[3]

MacGregor noted that some of those men who were left behind had earlier behaved themselves with great courage and discipline. "I think it but justice to express my belief," he said, "that the same difficulties which had nearly proved fatal to Captain Cobb's personal escape, were probably found to be insurmountable by landsmen, whose coolness, unaccompanied with dexterity and experience, might not be available to them in their awful situation." He also added that "the exertions of Mr Muir third mate, were also most conspicuous during the whole day."

Captain Cook remained standing by the burning hulk at a respectful distance until about 1:30 a.m on the 2nd, when the long anticipated explosion took place.

> After the arrival of the last boat, the flames, which had spread along the upper deck and poop, ascended with the rapidity of lightning to the masts and rigging, forming one general conflagration, that illumined the heavens to an immense distance, and was strongly reflected upon several objects on board the brig. The flags of distress, hoisted in the morning, were seen for a considerable time waving amid the flames, until the masts to which they were suspended successively fell, like stately steeples, over the ship's side. At last, about half-past one o'clock in the morning, the devouring element having communicated to the magazine, the long threatened explosion was seen, and the blazing fragments of the once magnificent *Kent* were instantly hurried, like so many rockets, high into the air, leaving, in the comparative darkness that succeeded, the deathful scene of that disastrous day floating before the mind like some feverish dream.[4]

The *Cambria* was about three miles distant from the *Kent* at the time of its explosion. To his father, MacGregor admitted that "The unhappy men who were still on board, were now seen climbing up the rigging, and their yells as the fire approached nearer became quite unearthly. A speedy termination was put to their sufferings. The magazine, which was inundated early in the day, had at last been dried up—the fire reached, the explosion took place, the firmament was filled with the fragments of the once beautiful *Kent*, the sky was in a blaze for a moment, and next all was darkness."[5] Townsend, who watched the scene from the *Cambria*'s stern window, noted that "an involuntary shriek of horror burst from the spectators, and formed the climax of the mournful scene."[6]

Thomson published an account of his own in the newspapers, and more detail of the abandonment of the wreck was included in MacGregor's narrative as an appendix. Thomson said that he did not leave the *Kent* until after midnight when he was driven away by flames erupting from the gunroom ports and cabin windows. At that time, says the author of MacGregor's appendix, "the spanker-boom was crowded with soldiers. Such was their terror that even the greater, but less immediate, threat of the fire, and the prospect of being left, were not enough to overcome their fears of leaping from that height into the water." This account suggests that the rope from the end of the spanker boom had gone, but in any case the difficulty was that those with the courage to climb down it were unable to get past the clinging bodies of those who lacked that courage.

However, that was not the end for the men who had been unable to find the courage or skill to climb out the spanker boom and down the rope into the boats. Cannon's regimental history suggests that there were twenty still on board, probably not counting Sergeant Jack's four children hiding in Colonel Fearnon's cabin. But the number was somewhat more than that, and later testimony suggests that it was only the failure of the boats to return for one last time that condemned them to the final fiery end of the *Kent*.[7] If they had been intoxicated, their circumstances were such as to sober any man.

MacGregor never received an entirely clear story from the four-teen last survivors when he sought them out on their return to England, although he did not believe that they deliberately misled him. The author of the account given in the appendix to his narra-tive concluded that after the departure of the last boat, "they were driven by the flames to seek shelter on the chains, where they stood until the masts fell overboard to which they then clung for some hours in a state of horror that no language can describe."[8]

The description provided by "a Liverpool Correspondent" for the *Times* paints the situation of the people left onboard the *Kent* in understandably dark hues.[9]

> It appears, that the men left on the wreck never, for a moment, imagined that they should be abandoned by their comrades to perish either by fire or water. The flames broke out, they state, about seven o'clock in the evening, at or near the main-mast, and instantly ran, with great rapidity, from stem to stern, scorching and burning dreadfully many persons who could not escape from the fury of the destructive element. The fire still continuing to increase, about nine o'clock the flames caught the rigging. At this awful crisis, as near as the poor fellows could guess, the *Cambria* appeared to be getting under way. All the officers and men had got on board the brig, except two sergeants, two cor-porals, about 50 privates, and seven helpless children, all of whom were abandoned to their fate. The *Cambria*, they state, was not, at this time, more than a quarter to half a mile from the Kent. As soon as they perceived her making sail, they instinctive-ly raised a shout of despair, calling upon their more fortunate comrades not to abandon them to that death which, to all human appearance, was inevitable, if they were left on the burn-ing wreck. The soldiers are quite convinced, that their cries for help, which derived strength from despair, must have been heard

on board the *Cambria*. No notice, however, was taken of them, and the vessel soon disappeared from their sight.

The correspondent evidently confused the numbers of those left on board with the total number who died from the fire and drowning.

The sensations of the multitude, at this awful juncture, may be more easily imagined than described. The whole range of the *Kent* was now enveloped in flames, with the exception of part of the quarter-deck, which was the last to fall a prey to the furious element. The unfortunate wretches were now successively driven from place to place on the deck by the progress of the flames. Many affecting incidents occurred, during the dreadful interval between the departure of the *Cambria* and the time when the survivors were compelled, by the ravages of the flames, to commit themselves, as the only remaining chance of escape, to the fragments of floating wreck. Two brothers, named Berton, privates in the 31st Regiment, despairing of all hope of escape from the fiery element, affectionately embraced each other, and, joining hands, precipitated themselves into the sea. They both perished.[10] A father, whose wife, with one child, had got on board the *Cambria*, was left with a second child on the wreck. When the progress of the fire had rendered stay on board the *Kent* impossible, he threw himself and his helpless offspring into the sea, in the hope of being able to swim with it to some of the floating wreck. Unfortunately, the poor fellow could not keep his hold of his child, and it sunk from his paternal grasp to rise no more. . . . Another father had lashed his child to his back, and committed himself to the ocean with a similar object. The child perished, from the severity of the weather and the effects of the sea; and the unhappy father was reluctantly compelled to suffer its lifeless body to sink. Poor fellow! He soon afterwards shared the fate of his child. Many who had escaped the fury of one element, in despair precipitated themselves into the other, and perished.

The survivors, whose numbers had, by this time, been greatly diminished, had got on the booms, and some, we believe, on the yards, in the hope of thereby prolonging (for they had long abandoned all hope of escape) a miserable existence. Between 11 and 12 o'clock, the main and mizen masts fell overboard. The mizen mast floated away; whilst the mainmast—all the rigging not being entirely consumed—was fortunately prevented by a rope or ropes, from immediately leaving the hull, and it remained, rolling about, under or near to the stern. When the mizenmast fell overboard, there were about 16 unhappy men on the spanker boom, which, giving way at the same time, the whole of them were precipitated into the sea. Of these, one only succeeded in reaching the wreck of the mainmast. Several, however, from other parts of the vessel, reached and clung to it.

At this dreadful crisis, the *Kent* was one mass of flame, and presented an awful spectacle to the poor wretches doomed to behold the conflagration. Many unfortunate men had perished in attempting to reach the mainmast. Others, who had clung to different pieces of floating wreck, becoming benumbed, were unable to retain their hold, and sunk to rise no more, whilst others were drifted to leeward, and perished in the ocean. One or two of the yards of the mainmast were, fortunately, standing, and afforded a holding for those who got near it. From 10 to 12 of them clung to the round-top, whilst others fastened themselves along the mast or on the yards. Their bodies were nearly wholly immersed in the ocean, which was violently agitated, the waves making a complete breach over them, and the rolling of the mast adding to the difficulty of holding on.

The cold and the water benumbed the bodies and limbs of the poor men, and made them almost insensible to feeling. They were, too, nearly naked, the suddenness of the accident not allowing them time to clothe themselves. All this time the most to which they clung was rolling about under the stern of the ship, frequently within five yards of the wreck. The heat from the flaming hull was sensibly, and even gratefully, felt by the unfortunate men, warming them after the sea had washed over them, and preserving their bodies form total inanimation.

About two o'clock, the *Kent* blew up, with an explosion not remarkably loud, in consequence of most of the powder having been destroyed by sea-water which had inundated the magazine. Several fragments of the ship fell on the survivors on the mast, but they were fortunately, too small to injure them. One of the men thinks that a few dead bodies fell into the sea, having been blown up with the decks. The hull of the *Kent* still continued to burn on, the flames illuminating, by their dreadful glare, the surrounding scene of desolation. By half-past two, the fire had reached nearly to the water's edge; and the wretched survivors began to be apprehensive that they would be drawn into the vortex which her sinking would cause, and perish with her in the abyss.

The discrepancy between the testimony of these men, who had actually been onboard the wreck when the explosion occurred, and that of the witnesses onboard the *Cambria*, is not inconsistent with other experience. Frequently those near an explosion do not hear it, or hear it less loudly than do those at a distance.

The evidence taken by Colonel Fearon, in its understatement, evokes the full horror of the situation. In response to the questions of his commanding officer, Sergeant Benson said that when he left in what he believed was the last boat "the men on the boom called after them, but the boat could not contain more with safety." This does not square with Captain Cook's testimony that the last boat returned with only one man, but it is impossible to know for sure what actually happened. Corporal Peter McGowan said that when the boat left with Benson onboard, he "was on the spanker boom next to Thompson of the Grenadiers." When "they found there was no appearance of its returning, the whole of the men on the boom crept back upon the poop, where they remained, till the fire made such progress, that they were obliged to have recourse to the boom again, where they continued till it separated from the mast in consequence of the fire, when they fell into the water with it."[11]

McGowan estimated that there were "about 14 men on the boom; among whom were Serjeant Curry, Lawrence Feelay with his child tied to his back in a blanket, Thompson and others, whose names he does not know, all of whom were drowned with the exception of himself." He swam to the mainmast that had fallen overboard. Private Samuel Hassells was already clinging to it, and together they got into the round top. They were joined there by Private William Reynolds who "slung himself by a rope from the vessel and walked along the yard arm till he reached the round top." Private Thomas Fishwick cut what he thought was the only shroud connecting the mast with the wreck of the *Kent*, so that it would not be pulled under when she sank. But fortunately for them, given what was to follow, the wreck remained close alongside all the same.

Concluding his evidence, McGowan remembered that "the magazine made little or no explosion," and that "the guns only made a report as the fire reached them. . . . Several of the men perished when the guns went off by the fire dropping upon them on the rafts; he thinks he saw six in this way lose their lives," including privates William Haslam and John Develin. Private George Burton "jumped overboard and was drowned. . . . There was a sailor and two marine boys on the spanker boom besides the soldiers; they all perished." In all, he believed there had been about 30 men on the poop after the departure of the last boat. Samuel Hassells's testimony largely confirmed that of McGowan, and added that Private Andrew McIntyre had joined those clinging to the mast, but was washed off by a swell and sank.

"Out of the depths I cry to you, O Lord; Lord hear my voice." The words of Psalm 130 would have been familiar to all, and indeed the miracles were not over. "Relief was near at hand," concluded the *Times* Liverpool correspondent. Around three o'clock in the morning the men in the water "descried, with sensations of joy which we cannot attempt to describe, a vessel rounding, at a short distance, the burning hull of the *Kent*. They instantly and simultaneously set up as loud a shout as their enfeebled state would permit, in order to attract the attention of the crew. The vessel proved to be the *Caroline*, Captain Bibby, of this port."

Brig and Cutter Off the English Coast by Thomas Butterworth, c. 1815. (*Vallejo Gallery*)

7

Caroline

MacGregor was not an eyewitness of the *Caroline*'s rescue of the last of the regiment, still clinging to life onboard the *Kent*. Whoever wrote the account in the appendix to his narrative which appears to have been taken from the *London Magazine* was familiar with ships and the sea:

> About twelve o'clock at night on the 1st of March last, a bright light was observed in the horizon by the watch of the bark *Caroline* on her passage from Alexandria to Liverpool, proceeding apparently from a ship on fire. It having blown strong the preceding day, the *Caroline* was at the time under double reefed main and fore-top sails, main trysail, and fore-top-mast stay-sail, close upon a wind with a heavy sea going. Word was immediately passed to Captain Bibby, who instantly bore up, and setting his main top gallant sail, ran down towards the spot.[1]

The *Caroline* had been built in Prince Edward Island in 1821, on the north side of Hillsborough River, for Duncan MacKay, a

Charlottetown merchant. As was usual with Prince Edward Island ships, MacKay had only owned her for a single voyage to Liverpool, where she proceeded under the command of Alexander MacDonald.

The *Caroline* was 95 feet five inches long, had a beam of 26 feet eight inches, two masts and a trysail, two decks, and a height between decks of five feet six inches. She was described by the Liverpool tide surveyor, Henry Chad, when she was re-registered with Liverpool owners on April 1, 1822, as a square sterned brig with no galleries. She was rated as being of 281 and 45/94ths tons, based on having a length of keel of 24 feet five inches. But that dimension was only an approximation, as she was measured while afloat. By a curious irony, the figureheads of all three ships, the *Kent*, *Cambria*, and *Caroline*, were all described as representing "a woman's bust." But sailors being what they are, the selection of a female form for a figurehead was by no means unusual.

The *Caroline* had passed rapidly through a succession of owners, changing hands again on April 16th, October 22nd, and October 23rd, when she passed into those of John Askew of Liverpool. Robert Bibby was given her to command on October 29, 1822, but he does not appear to have ever been an owner.[2] A search through the 1841 and 1851 censuses discovers a Robert Bibby who was born in Crosby, Lancashire, about 1791, and had by 1841 made his home in Wirrall in Cheshire, across the river from Liverpool. That would have made him 34 in 1825.[3] His wife's name was Elizabeth, and her age in 1825 would have been 24. She was a girl from Wigan, but the only marriage record for a Robert Bibby is one dated 1823 in Assington, across England in Suffolk to an Elizabeth Wright.[4] The muster certificate sworn in Bibby's absence in Liverpool on April 16, 1825, after the hands had been discharged, indicated the *Caroline* had a crew of 19 men, all of whom were stated to be Liverpudlians.[5] In March 1825, she was on her voyage home from Alexandria in Egypt with a cargo of cotton.[6]

The lookout on the *Caroline* sighted the fire at the same time as Captain Cobb finally set his course to take the *Cambria* toward England.

> About two o'clock [in the morning], when every eye was intensely fixed upon the increasing brightness in the sky, a sudden jet of vivid light darted upwards, evidently caused by an explosion, though they were as yet too far distant to hear any report. In half an hour the *Caroline* had approached sufficiently near to make out the wreck of a large vessel, lying head to wind, of which nothing remained but the ribs and frame timbers, which, marking the outlines of a double line of ports and quarter galleries, afforded too much reason to fear that the burning skeleton was the remnant of a first class East Indiaman, or a line-of-battle ship. The flames, however, had so completely consumed every other external feature, that nothing could be ascertained with accuracy. She was burned nearly to the water's edge; but becoming gradually lighter as the internal timbers and fallen decks and spars were consumed, she still floated, pitching majestically as she rose, and fell over the long rolling swell of the bay. Her appearance was that of an immense cauldron or cage of buoyant basket-work, formed of the charred and blackened ribs, naked and stripped of every plank, encircling an uninterrupted mass of flame, not, however, of uniform intensity, as from two or three points, probably where the hatch ways had supplied an additional quantity of looser fuel, brighter emissions were bursting upwards. Above, and far to leeward, the atmosphere was a cloud of curling smoke, the whole sprinkled with myriads of sparks and burning flakes of lighter materials, thrown up without intermission, and scattered by the wind over the sky and waves.[7]

The correspondent for the *Times* said that the *Caroline* sailed 20 miles before she came close to the hulk, and that Captain Bibby had to be careful about his approach because he had a deck cargo of cotton which a spark might ignite. Keeping a safe distance, "he very judiciously and skillfully ran to leeward of the ship, to allow any person who might be in boats or on pieces of the wreck an opportunity of more easily and safely getting on board the *Caroline*."

As the *Caroline* bore down, part of a mast and some spars were observed rising and falling, and almost grinding under the starboard, or what might be called the weather-quarter of the wreck; for although, as has been stated, it rode nearly head to wind, in the course of drifting, these spars being fast to the after-part in some degree, gave the stern-frame a slight cant to windward.

The *Caroline* coming down right before the wind was, in a few minutes, brought across the bows of the wreck, and as near as was consistent with safety. At that moment, when, to all appearance, no human being could be supposed to retain life within the sphere of such a conflagration, a shout was heard, and almost at the same instant several figures were observed clinging to the above-mentioned mast and spars. From their low situation, almost upon a level with the water, and the rapidity of the bark's motion, she could not have been visible long before they hailed—what then must have been their feelings, when (no rational hope of rescue remaining)—they suddenly beheld within a few yards the hull and sails of a large vessel, brilliantly illuminated by the glare. But whatever those feelings were, a fearful pause ensued, for, with equal rapidity, gliding athwart the bows of the *Kent*, the stranger disappeared, leaving them to their conjectures as to the possibility of being saved, even if the attempt were made, in consequence of the heavy sea, and probable disappearance of the wreck before a boat could reach them.[8]

Captain Bibby quickly summed up the situation, the peril to his own ship and the mortal danger to the men in the water, and without hesitation knew what he should do. He ordered his crew to take in the topgallant sail, lower the fore topmast staysail, and continue the course under topsails and trysail to leeward, keeping at a distance to avoid the danger of falling flakes and sparks, but at the same time, near enough to make it possible to send a boat to rescue the men. When he had reached his position, the fore topsail was braced aback, and the vessel hove to. As the *Times* correspondent noted, the leeward position was chosen so that, were it possible for the men in the water to cut their improvised raft off from the wreck, they would drift down wind towards safety. In the sea that was running, only very well handled boats could be expected to row to windward.

Bibby ordered the *Caroline*'s jolly boat lowered from the stern davits, and the mate, Matthew Wallen, took charge of her and a crew of four oarsmen. A boat of that size and with only four at the oars was very vulnerable in a heavy sea. The *Times* correspondent described it as being only 14 feet in length, but the later report in the MacGregor narrative gave the more probable length of 18 feet, although of an "inferior design." The danger was made infinitely greater by the debris thrown into the sea when *Kent* exploded. The litter of broken spars, casks and cases, was rolling in the troughs of the sea, and tossing to the summit of the waves ready to crash down on the approaching boat.

The seamanship of these Liverpudlians was of the highest order.

Having approached within a few yards of the stern, they caught sight of the first living being; a man was observed writhing as he clung to a rope or portion of wreck close under the ship's counter—so close, indeed, that, as the stern-frame rose with the swell, he was jerked upwards, and suspended above the water, to meet a more dreadful fate, for, with few and short intervals, streams of pure flame gushed forth through the casings of the gun-room ports, and scorched the poor sufferer, whose cries of agony they could distinctly hear, and which only ceased when, as the surge passed on the descending stern-frame, plunging downwards it buried him in the waves.[9]

The danger for the *Caroline*'s boat's crew in trying to approach this man was enormous, but the thought of leaving him to his fate did not delay mate Wallen, who wrote, "He appeared to be the worst off, and therefore the first it was our business to look after." But that was not to be. He had already fallen silent when the *Caroline*'s boat drew near, and before it could reach him, the rope or spar connecting him to the *Kent* burned through. He instantly sank and did not resurface. Wallen then backed the jolly boat toward the floating mast, and despite the swell, managed to recover six men.

To have taken more would have risked the safety of the whole; for it may be easily conceived that in a small merchant's jolly-boat, about eighteen feet in length, and in many respects inferior to the generality of boats of this description, eleven persons in a heavy sea, and under such circumstances, were even more than it was consistent with strict prudence to carry, and, in fact when returning, they were warned, by a heavy wave which nearly swamped them, of the consequence of overloading so small a conveyance.[10]

In his evidence to Colonel Fearon, Samuel Hassells's memory of how long the remaining men maintained their grasp on the *Kent*'s spars is confused, but he recalled that he was the first that let go and swam to get onboard the *Caroline*'s boat. Fishwick added the poignant detail that he "was on the poop, when the last boat left the vessel, with his child tied to his back; he afterwards came back to the poop with his child, and sat down for some time there till the flames reached him, when he got over the side, and clung on there for some time, till the fire coming out of the cabin windows and ports, he drop'd the child into the water, and went after it; he swam and caught hold of a boom, by which he got to the round top of the main mast." Fishwick's child was one who died.

If possible, Private William Reynolds's story was yet more grim. He was the one MacGregor had noticed being lowered into one of the boats with three children tied to him—his own, Sergeant Murray's, and Sergeant Curry's—but he did not reach safety because the rope holding the boat to the *Kent* had broken, and he was eventually hauled back onboard. He remained on the poop until the spanker boom fell into the sea and then went "to the wind-ward side and sat down the blanket around him and the child dead in his arms; the fire then caught the place where the hammocks used to be put, and was communicating to the blanket, when he took it off, and left the child wrapt in it upon the hen coop." He climbed down into the mizzen chains with "about twenty others," but when the mast fell it created a sea anchor, and the *Kent* turned into the wind. The fire then searched out the men in the chains, and Reynolds used one of boat falls to swing clear of the wreck, where he could swim to the mast. He said that John Robinson and William Simmonds were with him, and that he persuaded John Develin to come as well, but that Develin drowned in the attempt. Seeing that Peter McGowan was nearly exhausted, Reynolds changed places with him, and believed he had thereby saved his life. When the *Caroline*'s boat arrived, Reynolds was the fourth to get into it.[11]

It took half an hour for the jolly boat crew to recover the first six men, after which Wallen immediately returned to the wreck. It took longer this time because the *Caroline*, although hove to, was drifting to leeward faster than was the wreck. Wallen had not seen any survivors, apart from those on the mast under the weather-quarter of the wreck, and so he returned there and managed to take off another six.

It looked as though the burning wreck was about to sink, and it was evident to Wallen that the situation of those remaining on the spar was becoming increasingly desperate. This posed the double threat that suction around the sinking hull would draw the men beneath the waves, and that with the extinction of the flames, all hope of seeing them in the dark would be gone. In the race against time the jolly boat crew crossed the longer distance to the *Caroline* in no more time than they had taken in the first trip, but luck ran out before they could return to the survivors on the spar, heaving on their oars against the head sea.

Before they could reach the mast, the anticipated and dreaded event took place. The fiery pile was observed to settle slowly on the waves, and gradually disappear. In another instant, the hitherto bright and burning atmosphere was involved in utter darkness, rendered still more awful by the contrast; a dense cloud of black smoke lingered like a shroud over the spot, and to the loud crackling of burning timbers and rustling of flames) a death-like silence had succeeded.

As the last of the flames disappeared below the sea, Wallen noted a star directly over the spot, to guide him back to where the men might be still struggling in the water. But for the moment he did not dare attempt to take the jolly boat through the floating wreckage in the dark. The danger to all in her was too great when

"When Day Broke the Mast was Visible," from the 1885 edition of MacGregor's narrative.

there was no chance of avoiding collision. Instead, the men rested on their oars for over an hour awaiting dawn. To comfort the wretched survivors, they shouted into the darkness, and eventually heard a faint shout in return, which they answered with a loud three cheers. Wallen kept his eye fixed on the star all the while.

When dawn broke, four bodies were seen among the mass of cordage and spars, but they were motionless. Only when they approached closer did two of them raise their heads and stretch their arms toward the approaching boat. Wallen carefully backed toward them so that they could be pulled over the transom and laid in the bottom of the boat; they were in a state of complete exhaustion. The other two showed no sign of life. One had attached himself firmly to the spar and grasped it in his arms, resting his head upon it "as if in sleep." The other stood half upright between the cheeks of the mast, with his arms extended, and his face turned toward the direction of the boat. Both were dead. It was too dangerous to attempt to recover the bodies. The crucified corpse, and the sleeper, were left in the ocean graveyard.

An attempt was made to recover one of the *Kent*'s abandoned boats, in which it was thought some survivors might be found, but it was empty and had to be abandoned when the weather took a decided turn for the worse. At dawn the sky to windward took on a sinister appearance, the wind began to squall, and the seas, which during the night had been long, began to crest, and to break along their top. Not a moment could be wasted. It seems probable that had the jolly boat not returned to the *Caroline* when it did, it might have been impossible to recover it, and its brave crew and the last two survivors would have been lost.

It is not unlikely that there were men still clinging to spars that had drifted to leeward. MacGregor thought that Captain Bibby considered waiting until full daylight to search for more survivors, but that is unlikely. "Every prospect of preservation being thus annihilated," concluded the author, "we can only hope that, in such a state of utter despair, the sufferings of these wretched beings were not long protracted. The humanity and meritorious efforts of Captain Bibby and Mr. Wallen are above all praise, and well deserve to be extensively known."

The *Times* correspondent completed the story.

The poor fellows were lifted by the seamen out of the boat into the *Caroline* as they arrived, and carried, like helpless children, to the fire. Captain Bibby had them immediately stripped, and dry clothing put on their enfeebled and worn-out bodies. He ordered the cook to make some coffee, which he gave them to drink. This beverage revived their exhausted and languid frames. They were afterwards put into the best place that could be prepared for them, and they soon fell into a sound sleep, from which they awoke greatly revived and strengthened. Substantial food was then given to them, and they gradually recovered their wonted health and strength. . . . The same beneficent Providence which had been so wonderfully exerted for the preservation of hundreds, was pleased by a still more striking and unquestionable display of power and goodness, to avert the fate of a portion of those few who, we had all too much reason to fear, were doomed to destruction.

Bibby shaped his course to round Land's End at the extreme west of Cornwall, in order to complete his intended passage to his home port of Liverpool. On March 9th, the *Caroline* was reported in the *Liverpool Courier* entering Liverpool quarantine ground.[12]

Falmouth Harbor, from an early nineteenth-century engraving.

8

Landfall

BAY OF BISCAY TO FALMOUTH HARBOR,
MARCH 2–4, 1825

IT WAS FORTUNATE THAT THE *Cambria* had not been carrying cargo on her lower deck, instead of having it clear for the Cornish passengers. This circumstance made it possible to cram the survivors into the little brig, in great discomfort, but in safety and many of them out of the weather. Had it been necessary to throw the cargo overboard for this purpose, in the prevailing sea condition, the task might have been found impossibly dangerous. It was also fortunate that the *Cambria* was on her outward voyage and had just cleared her port, because she had all her ship's stores nearly intact. All the same, stores which were intended for a crew of 11 and a passenger list of 31 could not provide for the additional numbers from the *Kent* for many days.

Without hesitation, Captain Cook turned before the southwesterly gale and ran back into the approaches to the Channel, toward Falmouth. Any delay could have reduced the ship to a state of starvation, but too much haste risked damage to the little brig, from torn canvas, broken spars, or even being swamped by a following sea breaking over the stern. MacGregor conceded that it "would have been madness" for Cook to have kept the *Cambria* hove to until daybreak, as he believed Captain Bibby did the *Caroline*.

After the first congratulations, and "becoming acknowledgment of the Divine mercy," the survivors were inclined to fall silent, and reflect on their experiences. They did not appear to be fully alive to their continued danger. So great was the relief at having survived the fire, and finding their loved ones, that few seemed to fully understand that their situation was critical and could become disastrous.

Over 600 people were crammed together in a 200-ton brig, in a heavy gale, with several hundred miles of sea between them and a safe port. The cabin MacGregor found himself in was intended for at most ten people, but into it were crammed nearly eighty. In his letter to his father he said that

> there was no room for lying down, nor were many of us permitted to take up the room of sitting except by turns; and most of us, I believe, stood up for two days and three nights without closing an eye, and in a heavy gale of wind. Some children died of exhaustion on board, and I verily believe that had we remained twenty-four more hours longer in the brig, that many must have expired. Our situation in some respects was worse if possible than in the *Kent*. The baby's tongue and mouth were white as paper with the thrush, and since our arrival, medical men say that he could not have lived many hours longer on board. Elizabeth had no milk for him, and from the crowded state of the vessel and the violence of the gale, no fire could be made to heat water.[1]

He was fed only on a little sugar, and cried incessantly. In the 1820s, it was taken for granted that women needed to be provided with greater comfort, but none was available. More serious was the lack of air. With a height between decks of 5 feet 2 inches, there would not have been any air circulation over the heads of the standing bodies. Because of the damage that had been suffered to the *Cambria's* bulwark, waves continually broke over the deck, and to prevent the water flooding into the hull, the hatches had to be kept shut. MacGregor says they were only lifted "between the returning waves, to prevent absolute suffocation below, where the men were so closely packed together, that the steam arising from their respiration excited at one time an apprehension that the vessel was on fire; while the impurity of the air they were inhaling became so marked, that the lights occasionally carried down amongst them were almost instantly extinguished." Townsend told his sister that the conditions were "as if on a slave ship."[2] How Captain Cook managed to station men to open the hatches between waves is not at all clear, and no mention was made in any of the accounts of latrine arrangements, if indeed any could be contrived.

Many of the survivors could only be accommodated on the weather deck, where they were cold, wet, and some, who had been surprised in bed or had taken off their clothes in order to swim to the boats, nearly naked. All were standing ankle deep in the water that rushed over the planking. Some of the women and children were reduced to hysterics or fits, and like Elizabeth's baby John, the soldiers' babies could not be fed by their exhausted and famished mothers. The woman who gave birth several hours after being brought onboard, Mrs. Kuff, appropriately named her new son Cambria, and it is a wonder that both mother and child survived the ordeal.[3]

But wild as was the ride, the gale was now their friend, driving them northeastward toward safety. Despite the risk, Captain Cook crowded on sail. Townsend told his sister they made 9 knots an hour. Should the pressure on the masts cause one to break, the fate of all on board would have been a brutal end from famine and pestilence, but it would be no less disastrous were they to be becalmed before reaching port. Evidently the *Cambria*'s masts were sound, and Captain Cook knew just how much they could take. Racing before the wind, he had to be vigilant that a following sea did not develop and crash down over the stern.

Two days and three nights in the conditions onboard the *Cambria* is a very long time, but such was the exhaustion of the survivors that the time may have seemed dreamlike. The mothers and fathers with babies and small children would have had a particularly anxious time, but exhaustion can dull even that stress, and the pain of those bereaved. It was only Captain Cook and the crew of the *Cambria* that needed to remain alert, and for them there may have been little opportunity for sleep except on a deck swept by the spray whipped off the tops of waves. Watches would change in the established routine every three or four hours, but there would have been no place to go when relieved at the helm or lookout. The wind continued to increase, but masts and sails remained intact, and Captain Cook's London crew did not break.

On the afternoon of the 3rd, the lookout at the masthead saw "Land a-head." In the evening, lights were seen on the Scilly Isles west of Land's End in Cornwall. But the *Cambria* faced another challenge. A total of 530 wrecks have been registered around the Scilly archipelago, of which the best known is Sir Cloudesley Shovell's flagship, HMS *Association*, which on October 22, 1707 ran aground on the Gilstone Ledges near Bishop Rock, with the loss of all on board, about 800 men. Three other ships of the fleet were also wrecked. And in 1798, HMS *Colossus,* escorting a convoy, sought shelter in the roads before the Island of St. Mary, but was wrecked when her anchor cable broke. With her was lost a large part of a collection of antique vases made by Sir William Hamilton, the British envoy to Naples, and husband of Admiral Nelson's mistress. The *Cambria,* however, safely passed the Scilly dangers, the Longships rocks off Land's End, and safely weathering the Lizard, the promontory east of Penzance Bay on which many ships had been driven. Once round the Lizard, the *Cambria* cleared the Manacle rocks to the northward, and entered Falmouth harbor between 12:30 and 1:00 a.m. Friday morning March 4th.

The circumstances that enabled most of the passengers and crew of the *Kent* to be brought onboard the *Cambria* and carried in such a short time to a safe harbor were certainly remarkable. MacGregor saw their survival as a clear indication of the hand of God. "If a single link in the chain had been withdrawn or withheld, we must all most probably have perished."

The *Cambria's* entrance into Falmouth harbor was only just in time. MacGregor tells us that within the hour the wind "chopped around" into the northwestward, and remained in that quarter for the next several days. The *Cambria* could have been forced to stay at sea, or even blown to the westward, and not been able to reach port for weeks. With the conditions prevailing onboard, the death toll would have been terrible. "One cannot help concluding," wrote MacGregor, "that he who sees nothing of a Divine Providence in our preservation must be lamentably and wilfully blind 'to the majesty of the Lord.'" Far away to the southward, *Scaleby Castle* had noted this same sudden change of the wind, three days before, on March 1st.[4]

THERE is some uncertainty about the number of survivors onboard the *Cambria* when she entered Falmouth harbor. Captain Cook's first estimation of the numbers saved, which he sent on March 4th to his agents at Lloyd's of London, were wrong in several respects. He numbered the regimental survivors at 301, but thought that only 46 women and 48 children had survived.[5] When later asked by the War Department, Cook said that the *Cambria* was carrying 295 survivors from the 31st Regiment, with their 53 women and 58 children, and 141 of the crew of the *Kent*.[6] The fourteen soldier survivors later brought in by the *Caroline* would have brought the number of soldiers to survive up to 309. If this is compared with MacGregor's statement of the number who boarded the ship at Gravesend and Deal, 20 officers, 344 soldiers, 43 women, and 66 children, belonging to the 31st Regiment; 20 private passengers, and the *Kent*'s officers and crew totaling 148 men and boys; it appears that seven of the crew and 55 soldiers died. In fact, the official War Department return of soldier deaths in the regiment listed 54 names.[7] It may be supposed that Cook included the six officers' wives and possibly Colonel Fearon's grown-up daughter among the 53 women he brought ashore. MacGregor's numbers must be corrected by the addition of the stowaway wife, and later by the birth of Cambria aboard the brig. That would leave only one woman dead, and we know that Mrs. Molloy died of smoke inhalation. It appears from MacGregor's numbers that 14 children died, if Cook had thought to include little Cambria and John MacGregor in his numbers. Two of them had died at the start of the voyage; the three Molloy children were killed by the smoke with their mother; we know of Sergeant Jack's four children, and those of Privates Fishwick and Reynolds, and Sergeants Murray and Curry. If the number of 14 children dead is correct, that would suggest that only one child died during the hellish days crammed into *Cambria*. But other accounts suggest that more than 14 children died; a note in Colonel Fearon's papers indicates that 18 perished.[8] Captain Bray gave the number as 20 children "of the regiment."[9]

As soon as Captain Cook was confident that the *Cambria* was safely moored, MacGregor hurried ashore to Pendennis Castle to inform Lieutenant Colonel W. Fenwick, its Lieutenant-Governor, of the necessity to disembark the survivors and find shelter for them ashore.[10] Colonel Fearon was unable to go ashore himself, no doubt because of his injured leg. Long before daylight, orders were given and word sent to Captain Andrew King, Royal Navy, who had recently retired from the Navy and was superintendent of the Falmouth Packet service. He requisitioned the necessary boats to bring everyone ashore.[11] The women and children were first into the boats, and so swiftly had the word of the disaster to the *Kent* got around that they were met by a large crowd. The *Times* reported that "although blowing a gale of wind, every hand was employed in landing them, which object, however, was not completed till six" Friday evening.[12]

The first report of the disaster appeared in the *Royal Cornwall Gazette* dated Falmouth, March 4th: "A more melancholy duty never fell to our lot than to relate the loss of the Honourable Company's ship *Kent*. . . . The scene at Falmouth quay was affecting beyond description: women lamenting the loss of their husbands and children, men of their wives, and children of their parents, and all were in a state of nakedness."[13] MacGregor was convinced that more than curiosity brought the populace to the landing place. Everything was needed, down to basic clothing, food, and shelter.

> The sailors and soldiers, cold, wet, and almost naked, quickly followed; the whole forming, in their haggard looks, and the endless variety of their costume, an assemblage at once as melan-

choly and grotesque as it is possible to conceive. So eager did the people appear to be to pour out upon us the full current of their sympathies, that shoes, hats, and other articles of urgent necessity, were presented to several of the officers and men, before they had even quitted the point of disembarkation. And in the course of the day, many of the officers and soldiers, and almost all the females, were partaking, in the private houses of individuals, of the most liberal and needful hospitality.[14]

Edward Bray says he "landed in a Sailors Jacket and a woollen nightcap on my head—which some kind sailor on the *Cambria* lent me. Mrs Bray had on a man's shirt and a night wrapper, and Miss C. Murray lay three days in the brig in her wet cloths—everyone alike lost all their property and a more deplorable sight could not have been witnessed than to see us landing cold, wet, and half naked."[15] It seems, however, that his two children survived the ordeal with their parents, so there was much to be thankful for.

In the forefront of the host of helping hands were the Society of Friends, "that peculiar sect of Christians," wrote MacGregor, "who have ever been as remarkable for their unassuming pretensions and consistent conduct, as for unostentatiously standing in the front ranks of every good work. And so strong is the reason which I in particular have to associate in my mind all that is sincere, considerate, and charitable, with the Society of Friends, that the very badge of Quakerism will, I trust, henceforward prove a sufficient passport to the best feelings of my heart."[16] Elizabeth, Duncan, baby John, and probably Joanna were taken in by William Crouch who was one of the Quakers. Bray says he and his wife were "taken to the house of Mr. Broad the agent for Lloyd's where we received every mark of the kindest hospitality. They received us not as strangers but as if we had been old friends."

When he was 90 years old the Reverend Frederick Trestrail wrote *The Short Story of a Long Life* in which he recollected that

Of course I did as others did and laid hold of the first person about my own size and took him into the Royal Hotel. He was so stunned by the calamity, so cold and stiff with having to keep in one position so long, that I had to wash him from head to foot. Happily my clothes fitted, and when he recovered a little he put his hand to his head and, in rich Cork brogue, exclaimed 'Whatever will become of my unfortunate pate?' I ran down to my hatter, got a nice foraging cap for him and then left to find some other like destitute person.

He added that

When Captain Cook came amongst them they all fell down on their knees. Some got hold of his hands, some of his feet and, with tears flowing down their cheeks, called in words eloquent, earnest and full of pathos 'The Blessing of heaven on his head.' He was perfectly unmanned and he stood there weeping like a child, but doubly grateful that he had been the means of saving so many from death.

   Some days after I received a note signed 'Edward Townsend MD,' urgently requesting me to come to breakfast with him at the Royal Hotel. On going thither I was greatly surprised to meet the gentleman I had clothed. He looked very differently, as you may suppose. He was greatly moved as we met.[17]

How reliable this memory may be is open to question, however. In his letter to his sister written a week after landing, Townsend said that he was given clothes by "Captain James and lived almost entirely at Pendennis Castle with Captain Hall from whose family I received the greatest kindness."[18]

The charity continued and became more organized when the inhabitants of the town called a public meeting, where they raised a subscription of money, and continued the collection of clothing. The women and children continued to be the first care, and in keeping with the standards of the time, mourning clothing was found for the widows and orphans. For the soldiers and private passengers, a depository was established where they could find shirts, shoes, and stockings. For the sick and wounded, mostly suffering from bruises and exhaustion, places were found in the hospital where they received medical attention, and were also "invited to partake freely of the most judicious spiritual consolation and instruction."

Edgecomb Rimmell said that "many opened their doors to receive the strangers, others supplied them with clothing, and satisfied their more pressing wants, while the ladies immediately commenced an active canvass for pecuniary aid; and never did youth and beauty appear so interesting as when they thus became the advocates of the destitute, and pleaded with artless and successful eloquence the cause of the 'fatherless children and the widow.'"[19] The *Times* Falmouth correspondent admitted that "the hospitality of Falmouth and its environs was fully proved by the grotesque appearance of the men, women, and children: some of the women dressed in flounces and furbelows, others in prim Quakers' shawls and caps; some of the officers with large great coats, and trousers rather small; some with shoes pinching their toes, and others with boots large enough for both legs. Our Penryn friends were not behind: a collection of clothing commenced at day-break, and a chest provided to convey it to Falmouth; but on bringing the whole together, it was found a cart would not contain it." The Falmouth Harmonic Society, helped by some of the 31st's band who had recovered sufficiently from their ordeal to play on borrowed instruments, performed a concert, which added £22 to the relief fund.[20]

At a public meeting in Falmouth on March 31st, the ladies committee was particularly mentioned: "Of the humane exertions of the ladies on this affecting occasion, your Committee feel it difficult to speak in terms of sufficient admiration. They were, indeed, unremitted!—nor can the reciprocal interest which has been excited between them and the objects of their benevolence, be soon forgotten." By that date, £643/11/6 had been subscribed by the citizens of Falmouth, Truro, Helston, Penryn, and St. Ives, with support from the East India Company, Messers Marjoribanks and Company, the managing owners of the *Kent*, and from a list of major donors which included the Barclay and Fox families. £242/4/0 had already been distributed by the ladies' committee, £354/18/0 by the gentlemen's committee, and £146/9/6 remained.[21]

The survivors were naturally concerned to inform their relatives of their safety and distress. Townsend wrote a quick note to his sister Mary on the 4th: "Thanks to Almighty God I have another opportunity of once more writing. I cannot be too grateful to the Almighty for the wonderful escape I have had and hasten to relieve your minds from any anxiety less the report of the loss of the ship should reach you before you heard of my being safe here. . . . Oh it is a terrible thing to be at sea in a gale of wind and in a ship in flames!"[22] Apart from MacGregor's to his father and Bray's to Loftus A. Bryan, we know of a letter from a private in the 31st, Daniel Collins, writing for himself and for his wife who also survived, which was addressed to a Mr. Steadhold in London, apparently a son-in-law. Having lost everything, he did not have money for a stamp, and obtained from Colonel Fearon a franc for free postage.[23]

James Hedderwick had been the curate of an inland village when his clerk, whose son was a sergeant in the 31st, heard the devastating news of the loss of the ship. "It was a considerable time before it was known who had perished, and who had been saved; and week afer week did the robust frame of the anxious parent become more and more feeble, and his grey hairs almost visibly heavier with sorrow." When at last word came that the man's son was safe, "the writer met, not far from the cottage, a group of villagers running and shouting as if, in truth, mad with joy. They were all too breathless to answer his inquiries: and as he looked across the fields, several other persons were seen hurrying on in the same joyous manner." Such was the fame that the sergeant acquired throught the counryside that "the daughet of an opulent farmer had much to do to secure him for herself, though her father offered him his discharge and a snug farm next his own." She succeded, and the sergeant-turned-farmer settled down to his new life.[24]

South East View of Kilkhampton Church. Cornwall. April 5th 1827.

Kilkhampton Church, Cornwall, sketched by John Chessell Buckler in 1827. The service for the *Kent* was probably held in the architecturally similar church of King Charles the Martyr, Falmouth. (*British Library*)

9

Home

THREE DAYS AFTER REACHING FALMOUTH, on Sunday March 6th, Colonel Fearon led all the officers and men of the 31st Regiment to a service of thanksgiving, and was accompanied by Captain Cobb, the ship's officers, and the private passengers of the *Kent*. They marched without the regiment's colors, which had been lost in the fire.[1] MacGregor found the scene "deeply impressive;" and expressed his hope that "many a poor fellow who listened, perhaps for the first time in his life, with unquestionable sincerity and humility, to the voice of instruction, will be found steadily prosecuting, in the strength of God, the good resolution that he may on that solemn occasion have formed." The regiment had suffered something close to 15 percent dead, but it was a crack regiment that had suffered far worse during the Peninsular war, and now it dealt with its pain in the way soldiers do, with solemn courage. "Great is the Lord, and greatly to be praised," chants the Church of England's *Hymn of Praise and Thanksgiving After a Dangerous Tempest*, "let the redeemed of the Lord say so: whom he hath delivered from the merciless rage of the sea."

On the same day, the former passengers of the *Kent* delegated Captain Sir Charles Farrington of the 31st to deliver a letter of appreciation to Captain Cobb. Written in fulsome terms, it expressed their gratitude for his hospitality prior to the outbreak of the fire, and their recognition of his calm competence in dealing with the disaster:

> If those qualities, so conspicuous in your conduct during the whole period of our awful suspense, were observed to change their complexion, from moment to moment, it was by their assuming a loftier and nobler character, as the imminence of our danger increased; and amid the vain counsel of some, and the noisy and conflicting suggestions of many on board, we could not but admire how calmly but promptly you improved every opportunity of preserving your ship, which the varying circumstances of our situation presented; how humanely and affectionately you lent your personal aid and valuable counsel in early removing from the scene of destruction the numerous helpless women and children belonging to the troops; and how obstinately you adhered to your vessel until every individual, whom despair did not incapacitate from attempting their escape, had quitted it.[2]

Captain Cook and the *Cambria*'s ship's company were also showered with the thanks of all concerned. It was reported in the *West Briton and Cornwall Advertiser* on March 11th that the officers of the 31st had decided to present Captain Cook with "an elegant cup of the value of £50," and another valued at £20 to Mr. Connolly, the mate. "It is also intended to have a medal struck, to commemorate the heroic conduct of the miners, to whose spirited resolve, in refusing to allow the seamen of the *Kent* to enter the *Cambria*, until they had rescued those left on board the burning vessel, the preservation of the lives of the far greater part of those saved, is to be attributed."[3] When the cups were presented, the *Kent*'s passengers reflected that "God, 'who in the midst of judgment remembereth mercy,' had designed your bark as an ark of refuge for us, and had commissioned you, sir, to the high and honourable duty of opening the door to take us in." The medals were not immediately available, but Messers Lucas and Parker of the Anglo–Mexican Association, "the other gentlemen on board your vessel," and the miners were not forgotten. "We should be guilty of a most unpardonable omission, if we refrained from confessing how deeply we feel indebted to the brave and kind-hearted Cornish miners, who were proceeding on their passage to prosecute their industrious vocation in another hemisphere, for the very conspicuous and honorable part they bore."[4]

MacGregor says that, after the regiment returned to its barracks, due thanks were also sent to Captain Bibby for the part the *Caroline* had played in rescuing the last fourteen survivors. The first word of the arrival of the last survivors at Liverpool would have been that published in the *Times*, on March 11th, with the major article, headlined "The Kent East Indiaman," on the 17th.[5]

By that date, the 31st Regiment was again on the move. There was no time to waste if they were to resume their passage to India in the 1825 season. Immediately after his arrival in Falmouth, Colonel Fearon had informed the Commander-in-Chief at the Horse Guards in London, the Duke of York who was now 60, of the return of the regiment, and of its losses.[6] It was decided that it should be sent by sea to Chatham, and was embarked on the 13th.[7] It must have required a degree of resolution for them to trust themselves and their families once again onboard ship.

Colonel Fearon wrote to the Chairman and Members of the Relief Committee, thanking them for their assistance, employing the same high biblical language as MacGregor used in his published narrative. This was later published in the *Times*:

> We were thrown upon your shore as pennyless strangers, and ye took us in; we were hungry, and ye gave us meat—naked, and ye clothed us—sick, and ye relieved and comforted us. We have found you rejoicing with those of us who rejoiced, and weeping with such of us as had cause to weep. You have visited our fatherless and widows in their affliction, and sought, by unceasing acts of the most seasonable, effective, and delicate charity, to alleviate the measure of our sufferings. Under such circumstances, what can we say, or where shall we find words to express our emotions? You have created between us and our beloved country an additional bond of affection and gratitude, that will animate our future zeal, and enable us, amidst all the vicissitudes of our professional life, to point out Falmouth to our companions in arms as one of the bright spots in our happy land, where the friendless shall find many friends, and the afflicted receive abundant consolation.[8]

The temporary relief provided by the people of Falmouth, however, would not enable the survivors to avoid ruin if they did not obtain substantial relief. The survivors were all destitute, or nearly so. They had lost almost everything in the fire. MacGregor himself had only the gold sovereigns he had put into his wife's hand on her boarding the cutter, and a pocket-compass that his friend "E" had given him. In a schedule of losses suffered by individual officers, Colonel Fearon is shown as having lost £1,683/2/6; MacGregor £1,400; Captain Bray £1,200; and the rest between £300 and £600.[9] All of these are princely sums when it is considered that a loaf of bread cost a penny and a laborer's annual wages would not have exceeded £10. The soldiers could not even return to their duty without the money needed to replace their uniforms and equipment because the officers and men had had to provide for their own uniforms and camp equipage. The army recognized costs that ranged from £60 for a subaltern, with an additional £33 for the equipage to two subalterns, to £120 for a colonel and £80 for his camp equipage. The cost of a sergeant's uniform and equipage was £2/10/, and for a corporal, drummer, or private, £2/2/.[10] But the actual cost of the equipage needed for East India Service was considerably higher, and officers had to be able to pay the difference out of their own pockets. To do so, many of them had had to borrow money.

Bray wrote that "By this melancholy catastrophe I am reduced to absolute beggary—every shilling I possessed on the earth was expended on the purchase of everything requisite for a long residence in India—nothing is saved—all buried in the waves—nay more than all—for my exchange to the 31st caused me to contract a heavy debt which, had I gone to India, I could have soon repaid. Unfortunately for me, nothing was insured. Amidst my own ruin by loss of property and my prospects for life blighted forever, nothing presses more heavily on me than the loss of your two fine guns."[11]

The need was so great that Colonel Fearon appealed to the Duke of York. Lieutenant General Sir Herbert Taylor, the Secretary of Army headquarters at the Horse Guards, forwarded Fearon's letter to the Treasury Department, and also forwarded a subsequent Memorial addressed to the Chairman and Deputy Chairman of the Court of Directors of the East India Company: "The losses they have sustained amounts in many cases to the whole of their property, nay, in some has absorbed not only their property but also sums raised for the occasion to enable the individuals to fit themselves out and to provide accommodation for their families, and altho' ordered to prepare for embarkation and willing to obey the order at the shortest notice the greater part are quite unable to re-equip and resupply themselves."[12]

The Treasury eventually recognized a responsibility to provide for the costs involved at the official rate, but this fell short of actual requirements, and the Court of Directors acknowledged that, "on a consideration of the inadequacy for service in India of the rates of compensation granted to His Majesty's officers for the loss of baggage while on duty in the field, or when proceeding by sea under the orders of the government, they resolved several years ago to augment those rates very considerably." The company undertook to make up the king's allowance to subalterns from £60 to £113/15/, and that paid to Lieutenant-Colonel Fearon from £100 to £189/12/6, or if the king had not yet paid anything at all, to pay the full company allowance.[13] All the same, the total compensation paid him by king and company was only £214/12/6, while that for MacGregor was £238/3/.[14]

By the time that the soldiers had been informed of these payments they had left Falmouth. When they reached Chatham the officers were given hospitality by the Marines stationed there, who recalled that the 31st had once been Marines themselves.[15] They were then given ten days' leave. MacGregor seems to have spent his time writing his narrative, which is dated from London in April.

On March 18th, Joseph Dart was able to inform General Taylor that the *Charles Grant* was being provisioned for the transport of the officers and men of the 31st, with their wives and children: "She will be ready to receive the troops on board at Gravesend about April 2nd next, and the Court therefore direct me to request you will please to transmit me at an early opportunity a return of the number of officers and privates and also the families of the officers for whom passages will be required." Goodbyes had to be said again, and among Colonel Fearon's papers is a copy of his "Address on the Presentation of a Snuff Box by the Officers of the 31st Regiment to the Mess of the Royal Marines at Chatham." In return, the officers of the 31st presented the Chatham Division with a framed print of the loss of the *Kent*.[16]

It was found that there were only eight officers ready or willing to travel. Colonel Fearon did not re-embark with the right wing of the regiment, his place being taken by Lieutenant Colonel Cassidy.[17] Neither he nor his family were evidently in a hurry to board another ship for India. He spent some months in England, although his movements have not been traced with any exactitude. It was announced on April 2nd that he should be distinguished as a Companion of the Bath. Companions were not required to attend at Windsor, but he may have felt some need to be seen about town.[18]

Despite the fact that she was one of the largest of the Bombay-built Indiamen, it was determined that the *Charles Grant* only had space for 320 of the 378 other ranks and families. There was some embarrassment that the cabin stores that had been put onboard for the officers was now in excess of requirement, and could not be re-landed because of customs regulations.[19] Perhaps some of the excess comfort foods could have been put to good use by the less privileged who were not free to choose to remain ashore! It was evidently after failing to get a place in the *Charles Grant* that Anne Curry, having lost her husband and at least one child in the *Kent* disaster, petitioned the Governor of Chatham for assistance getting a passage to India with her two surviving sons. George and James Curry were both boy soldiers. It is pleasing to know that His Royal Highness, the Duke of York, asked the Court of Directors to provide for her on board the *Lord Hungerford* in which the regimental headquarters was transported to Calcutta under the command of a Major Francis Eagar, and it appears that James Curry accompanied her in that ship. George was the elder, and was promoted to private.[20]

One who did not board either ship for the passage to India was Sergeant William Molloy. It was popularly believed that he was stripped of his rank for abandoning his family in the fire, but in fact he was discharged on January 28, 1826, at the Royal Hospital, Kilmainham, as "being unfit for service, but able to earn a livelihood." He was awarded a pension of 6 pence per diem.[21]

On September 12th, after an uneventful passage, the two wings of the regiment were reunited at Berhampure, in India. Having gone into quarters at Fort William at Calcutta in November, it endured a terrifying outbreak of cholera. A replacement for the regimental colors burned in the *Kent* fire was presented on March 7, 1827 by Lady Amherst. For 21 years the 31st formed the garrison at Calcutta, broken by periods of very active campaigning in Afghanistan and the Punjab. When in 1841 the Afghans revolted against the puppet king, Shah Sujah, followed by the massacre in 1842 of the Kabul garrison as it withdrew through the Khyber Pass, the 31st formed part of the force sent to relieve Kandahar, and then recover control of Kabul. In the assault on the heights of Khourd Kabul Pass the 31st formed the advance guard, charging home with the bayonet, and sustaining heavy losses. The East India Company's flag returned to Kabul on September 15th, and Queen Victoria granted "Cabool, 1842," as a regimental battle honor. Three years later it was the Sikh war, and at a critical moment in the action at Ferozeshah against Lal Singh's army the Governor General, General Sir Henry Hardinge, rallied his men with the shout: "Thirty-First, I was with you when you saved the Battle of Albuera; behave like men now."[22]

Edward Bray commanded the 39th Regiment at the battle of Maharajpore on December 23, 1843. In the words of the moment in the garrison church at Aldershot, he "was desperately wounded in the last battery taken on that day, which was stormed by his regiment with the terrible loss in killed and wounded of 300 officers and men." His son, Ensign Theodore David Bray who had survived the *Kent* disaster, was killed in the same action, "while gallantly carrying the Regimental colour." John Clark in his nearly contemporary *History of India* wrote that "the Commander-in-chief and the officers of his staff had fallen into the usual error of despising the enemy, and considered them a contemptible rabble, ready to take to flight on the first shot. . . . Victory was at length secured, not by any professional skill, but simply by the irresistible gallantry of our soldiers, of whom a thousand fell killed and wounded."[23] Colonel Bray survived his son, and died on December 3, 1859, aged 74 years, having been made a Commander of the Bath. Belinda Bray died at Brighton on March 2, 1872, aged 74.

Among those who survived the Afghan and Sikh wars was private John Robinson who had clung to life in the wreckage of the *Kent* and been rescued by the *Caroline*. He was awarded the Cabul medal, and was discharged as "being worn out" in 1844. His discharge papers noticed that "He was onboard the *Kent* when she was lost at sea in 1825." He had married in India in 1830 and had a son before his wife died in 1839. Robinson had been a laborer before joining the 31st, and now he and his son retired to Ireland. The son became a tailor, but such was the dearth in Ireland that he was forced to sign up with the Honorable Company's army and return to India as a private in the Madras Fusiliers. He survived the Burma war of 1853–4, and the first relief of Lucknow in the Indian Mutiny, but died of dysentery on April 5, 1859. His father, however, was still alive in 1874 living in Newry, Ireland, and in receipt of a pension of 1/10d per diem.[24]

CAPTAIN Cobb had written to the Court of Directors as *Cambria* was rounding the Lizard before entering Falmouth harbor, but the first news they received of the loss of the *Kent* was a letter from John Carne, the company agent at Falmouth, dated March 5th. Carne's letter was read in the Committee of Shipping on Monday the 7th, by which time *Kent*'s purser, William Brown, had posted up to London and was waiting in the antechamber. No doubt his haste was increased by his financial interest in the stores for which he had accepted responsibility, and which had been lost.[25] When in 1837 regulations were published for the Indian Navy, it was indicated that the paymaster was to "withhold half of the purser's pay till his provision, store and cash accounts are sent in."[26] Brown was called into the Committee room, and questioned about the arrangements made by Captain Cobb at Falmouth for the destitute passengers and crew.

Mr. Kershaw, who had been the first to purchase a share of the *Kent*, was then called in to speak for her managing owner, Stewart Marjoribanks. He said that the owners were willing to implement any measures the Committee thought were appropriate for the relief of the survivors, and informed the Committee of Shipping about the Falmouth people's charitable activity. He also said that the owners would, if the Committee thought it appropriate, make arrangements to bring the survivors around to London by sea, and to cover the cost. "Mr. Brown and Mr. Kershaw then withdrew," noted the minutes, "and the Committee resolved, that Mr. Carne be desired to engage a conveyance by sea to London for the seamen belonging to the *Kent*, on as low terms as the same can be procured, and that he be also authorized to lay out one hundred guineas on the part of the company for the relief of the sufferers."[27]

The provision in the maritime law of the time, that British mercantile crews were not entitled to receive any pay unless they brought their ship safely into harbor and landed her cargo intact, left the *Kent*'s crew and their families without resources. Paradoxically, the company recognized the right of the ship owner to payment for freight prior to the destruction of the ship, but the seamen were owed nothing, and might even have lost their two months advance.[28] Rather than have them destitute on the London quays, however, Captain Cobb paid most of the *Kent*'s crew enough to see them to their homes, denying his generosity only to those who, according to MacGregor, "by their previously inhumane and insubordinate conduct, forfeited all claim to the slightest indulgence." Forty-nine of them also obtained financial assistance from the company agent at Plymouth. Captain Cook had reported to his insurance agents the poor performance of the *Kent*'s crew who manned the first cutter: "I cannot refrain from expressing my great disappointment of their conduct (in which I am borne out by Captain Cobb), derogatory in every respect to the generally received character of a British seaman, by refusing to return to the *Kent* for the people after the first trip, and requiring my utmost exertions and determination to compel them to renew their endeavors to get out the soldiers, passengers, and the remainder of their own shipmates who were left behind."[29]

The army and the company were quick to recognize an obligation to the men who had rescued the passengers and crew of the *Kent*. Upon learning that the *Cambria* was about to sail to resume her voyage to Vera Cruz, on March 9th, General Taylor wrote from the Horse Guards to thank Captain Cook on behalf of the Duke of York. "I am directed by his Royal Highness," wrote Sir Herbert, "to assure you of the high sense which his Royal Highness will not cease to entertain for the meritorious zeal and promptitude with which you came to the assistance of the ship *Kent*, under circumstances so critical and trying; and of the exemplary, gallant, and persevering exertions made by yourself and those acting under your direction, to which, under Providence, his Majesty and the country are indebted for the preservation of so many valuable lives."[30]

When the Committee of Shipping met on March 16th, it was able to read another letter from Mr. Carne expressing the thanks of the Falmouth Committee for the company's donation, and also indicating that a part of the *Kent*'s crew were already on their way to London, with the remainder soon to follow. The Committee of Shipping also received a letter from General Taylor, dated March 8th, expressing the concern felt by His Royal Highness the Duke of York, which provided a spur to further action. "Having maturely considered these documents," the Committee resolved to recompense the *Cambria* for the provisions Captain Cook had expended on the *Kent*'s crew, to a sum of £287/11/0, with an equal sum for "dieting" the passengers "during a detention of 25 days at £11 per diem." In addition, a Mr. Barker of the firm of Dobson and Barker of 144 Leadenhall Street, the *Cambria*'s shipping agent, was called before the Committee on behalf of the owners of the *Cambria*, when he indicated that they would be content with a payment of £300 for demurrage, the time the ship was not earning money in trade because it was either actively rescuing the *Kent*'s people, or was tied to a mooring in Falmouth.[31]

Neither was the Committee unresponsive to the heroism of the *Cambria*'s people. Without any reference to the declared intention of the officers of the 31st to strike a medal, the Committee also discussed the idea of presenting "to each individual who was onboard the *Cambria* a suitable medal as a mark of the general feeling of approbation which their most excellent & praiseworthy conduct in the late disastrous occasion has inspired." After Mr. Barker withdrew from the room, the Committee, "having further taken into consideration the very meritorious exertions of Captain Cook and his ship's company & passengers under the trying circumstances in which they were placed in rendering assistance . . . . Resolved to recommend to the Court that Captain Cook be rewarded with the sum of £600." The first mate was awarded £100, the *Cambria*'s carpenter who had stood as second mate was awarded £50, and the nine crewmen were each awarded £10. The 25 miners and smelterers, who were "of a superior sort," were each awarded £15. To this largess was added £100 with which Mr. Carne was to purchase cabin comforts for their voyage to Mexico.[32] The imputation is that "common" tin miners would have been undeserving of consideration. For some reason *Cambria*'s carpenter failed to receive his money and over a year later applied to Mr. Carne, whose letter to the Court of Directors was referred to the Committee of Shipping on December 13, 1826.[33]

The shower of money was added to by the Royal Exchange Assurance which paid Messers Dobson and Baker £50 as a present to Captain Cook, and another £50 to be divided between the officers and crew. The members of Lloyd's of London voted Captain Cook £100 and the Royal Humane Society awarded him, Captain Cobb, Colonel Fearon, and Major MacGregor Honourary Medallions. The citation took special notice of their "cool and intrepid conduct," the "danger of instant destruction from the explosion of the magazine of gunpowder," and their maintenance of "order and discipline among the troops under their command, so difficult to be enforced, but yet so essential to the successful issue of operations, conducted under such trying and disastrous circumstances." Captain Bibby and Mate Wallen were also awarded medallions.[34] The insurance underwriters at Liverpool also voted a sum of money but MacGregor did not know how much.[35] A miniature portrait of Captain Cook was painted by C.F. Thatcher, presumably after Cook's return to London later in the year because

Thatcher was then living in London at Cottage House, Paddington Green.[36] It is not known who commissioned the portrait, but it came to light in the late 1970s and was purchased by a descendant of Colonel Fearon's brother, Christopher Augustus.[37]

Inevitably, the disaster at sea led to an inquiry by the Committee of Shipping. This was scheduled for March 22. Campbell Marjoribanks vacated his deputy's chair because of the implications of the Committee's findings to his kinsman, Stewart, the ships's managing owner. Stewart Marjoribanks had indicated that he intended to build a new ship, "under the conditions of the Act of the 58 George 3rd Cap.83." which entitled him to build another ship, and claim the right to employ her for six voyages. But this provision would only be in force if there were not found to be any dereliction in the maintenance, supply, or operation of the ship that had been lost.[38]

Captain Cobb had by this time reached London, and had written on the 10th to indicate his readiness to give evidence to the Committee. He and the four senior mates were "called severely into the Committee, and were examined minutely respecting all the circumstance of the loss of the ship." Colonel Fearon had also been present and he "stated in very favourable terms his opinion of the conduct of Captain Cobb and his officers in the disastrous occasion." The Committee then adjourned until the 25th, when it examined McCray, the fifth mate, and Tighe, the sixth mate. It also took evidence from Major MacGregor who "spoke in the highest terms of the conduct of Captain Cobb and his officers."[39]

The direction taken by the Committee is indicated by a resolution to ask Sir Humphrey Davy, the inventor of the miner's safety lamp, whether his design would have prevented the *Kent*'s spilled spirits from igniting. They evidently also asked Captain Cobb if he could identify the work gang that had stowed the spirit barrels when the *Kent* was being laded in the Thames before sailing. But, "notwithstanding a diligent search," he said he had been unable to provide a list of names.

The Committee then took a break from its inquiries to read a letter dated March 19th from James Milligan, who was the company agent in Liverpool, reporting the arrival of the last fourteen survivors in the *Caroline*. "An occurrence took place here last week which though not immediately interesting to the company should perhaps have been more early communicated." "As soon as the *Caroline* was released from quarantine I went on board of her and saw the chief mate, Wallen, who was in the boat sent by Captain Bibby to inspect the wreck after the powder had exploded. He assured me there was not a seaman then to be seen and that the people who he was able to save were 14 soldiers, two other soldiers having died before they could be taken from the floating wreck, owing to the smallness of his boat. The soldiers," he added, "were this evening taken charge of by Captain Flinn, inspecting officer of this district, and well and humanely provided for."[40] Four days later the Committee received another letter from Liverpool enclosing one from Captain Bibby. Captain Bibby's letter is now lost, but it is possible it was the basis for the detailed account of the *Caroline*'s rescue work that was published in the *London Magazine* and which MacGregor placed in the appendix of his narrative. The Committee resolved to recommend to the Court that Captain Bibby and the crew of the *Caroline* should share a reward of £50, and that Bibby be requested to send an account of his expenses.[41] A month later, on April 27th, the Committee received an acknowledgment from Captain Bibby, after which it decided to increase its gratuity to

£100, so that Captain Bibby received £31/10/; the first mate £15/15/; the second £10/10/; the carpenter £5/5/; steward and cook £5 each; and the nine seamen £3 each.[42]

At the same meeting the Committee also considered a report forwarded by John Carne, with a doctor's certificate indicating that the Cornish wrestler, James Warren, who had worked so hard in the rescue of the *Kent*'s passengers, was "confined to his bed, and is likely to be a long sufferer." Colonel Fearon added his own recommendation, and Carne wrote that he had no doubt but that Warren's "great exertions were the means of saving a great number of persons from destruction on the occasion above alluded to: that he is now unhappily suffering from those exertions." The Committee resolved to award him the sum of 30 guineas, which would be more than enough to ensure him some comfort and provision while he was bed-ridden.[43] He was obliged to abandon his plan to be employed in Mexico, but he survived until 1842 when he died in St. Just on January 28.

THE question of whether some part of *Kent*'s crew might have been seeking to draw off some of the spirits during the storm may have been raised during the discussions of the Committee of Shipping, but if it were, the answers were evidently sufficiently convincing. On the 29th, "The Committee having maturely deliberated on the evidence adduced relative to the unfortunate destruction of the late ship *Kent* by fire and being unanimously of opinion that it appeared to have taken place from the accidental circumstance of the man dropping the lanthorn used, not from any want of proper precautions on the part of Captain Cobb or his officers as to the situation in which the spirits were staved, to whom the Committee cannot impute any blame, Resolved to submit to the Court their opinion that Captain Cobb and his officers should be fully acquitted of all imputation of neglect or misconduct in respect to the loss of the said ship." They also agreed that Stewart Marjoribanks had "fully and sufficiently found" the *Kent* with "all necessary anchors, cables, provisions and stores, and that the owners consequently should be fully acquitted of all imputation of neglect or misconduct in respect to the loss of the ship." Finally they agreed to submit "to the particular notice of the Court the evidence which has been given with reference to the coolness, intrepidity, and humanity evinced by Captain Cobb throughout the trying situation in which he was placed." The committee also recorded its appreciation of the part played by Colonel Fearon.[44]

A notice was placed in the *Times* datelined East India House, April 12, 1825. "The Court of Directors of the United Company of Merchants of England trading to the East Indies do hereby give notice, that at the General Court of the said company, appointed to be held at this House on Wednesday, the 27th Instant, the following resolution of the Court of Directors of the 30th Ultimo will be reported to the General Court, agreeable to the Act of 58th Geo III cap. 83, viz.: 'That it is the Opinion of this Court, that the commander and owners of the ship *Kent*, are fully acquitted from all imputation of neglect of misconduct in respect to the loss of that ship.' Joseph Dart, Sec."[45]

That judgment, at any rate, left Marjoribanks free to build a new *Kent*.

DESPITE the full exoneration granted by the Court of Directors, Captain Henry Cobb did not again command an Indiaman. On

February 14, 1827, the company's Committee of Private Trade accepted his resignation, noting "that the health of Captain Henry Cobb renders him unable to proceed in comand of the ship building on the bottom of the late ship *Kent*."[46] It should be borne in mind that captains frequently retired from East India Company service after three or four voyages having made their fortunes. The loss of the *Kent* would have reduced Cobb's fortune by his 1/16th share of its value, unless he had insured himself, but perhaps what he had left was enough to persuade him that he had no need to face another voyage. He does not disappear entirely, and the sequel makes it clear his illness was not of a fatal character. Thirty-seven years later, on November 1, 1862, Cobb wrote a letter to the *Times* in the capacity of treasurer of a committee that was raising money to reward the crew of the *Wave* of Colchester. In what the *Times* had described as "as gallant an action as was ever performed in the annals of the sea" the *Wave*'s people had effected the rescue off Newhaven of the master, crew and family of a small ship.[47]

OTHERS did return to sea. James Sexton, the *Kent*'s first mate, left almost immediately, serving as first mate in the East Indiaman *MacQueen* for her 1825–26 and 1827–28 voyages, and in the *Reliance* for her 1829–30 and 1831–32 voyages. His wife gave birth to James Middle on June 14, 1826, followed by Laura Louisa on February 28, 1832, and Ellen Susan on December 16, 1834. Basil William Muir, or Mure, was out of work for a year, but went back to sea as third mate of the *Duke of Sussex* for its 1826–27 voyage, rising to second mate in her for the 1828–29 voyage. But he died during that voyage, on June 16, 1829. John Hay served as second mate of the *Charles Grant*, and would have been a familiar face for the people of the 31st Regiment traveling in her, but not for long. He died on June 2, 1825 after she had been at sea less than a month. The heroic John Thomson, however, rose through the ranks to be first mate of the *Duke of York* in her 1830–31 voyage.[48]

A silver medal was indeed struck, apparently commissioned by the Falmouth committee, to commemorate the rescue of the *Kent*'s people. Designed by Thomas Halliday, the obverse shows a starboard broadside view of the *Cambria* hove-to with the *Kent* on fire to windward, with two boats plying between. The image was based on the work by William Daniell. Under the image was stamped the date March 1, 1825, and the legend on the reverse reads: "To Commemorate the Destruction of the Kent East Indiaman by fire, in the Bay of Biscay, and the Reception on board the brig Cambria, William Cook, Master, of 547 Persons, thus Providentially Delivered from Death." Halliday was a well-known Birmingham engraver who had his own establishment at Newhall Street between about 1810 and 1842. He engraved dies for the trade, but also engraved and manufactured tokens and medals at his own works.[49] It is believed that 50 or 60 were struck in silver to be presented to the leading actors in the drama, and each had his name struck on the rim of the medal presented to him. Several were also presented to the towns that had contributed to the relief effort, but no name was struck on those, and one was given to the East India Company in a ceremony presided over by the lieutenant governor of Pendennis Castle. An unknown number was also struck in copper and white metal to be sold as souvenirs, and the whole project may, in part, have been conceived as a fund raiser. If so, there has not been found any public advertising. The inscription engraved round the circumference of the legend side of the medal: "From Falmouth, Truro, Helston, Penryn and St. Ives," is consistent with the towns that contributed to it, but could also be the homes of the Cornish miners.[50]

COOK continued on his voyage to Mexico in command of the *Cambria*, but then took a year off, putting another in command. Little is known for certain about him, but there was a William Cook who gave his address at St. Mary Abbotts, Kensington, when he married Elizabeth Pierce at St. George's Hanover Square, Westminster, in 1826.[51] Perhaps the reward money, which totalled more than £900, had enabled him to move to a better address, and to marry, and perhaps his citation from the Royal Humane Society helped to persuade Elizabeth to accept his offer. He returned to sea in the *Cambria* between January and October 1827, but then retired from command. He continued to own his ship until November 16, 1830 when she was re-registered to another owner.[52]

FOR some reason, no one seemed interested in owning the *Caroline* for long. Ten days after her arrival in Liverpool, on March 19, 1825, Askew sold a half share in her to John Garnette, a Liverpool merchant. Captain Bibby left her after the crew was paid, and she was given to John Brothers and Smith on April 19, for harbor command. After the *Caroline* had been idle in Liverpool for more than a year, on December 5, 1826, a Peter Johnston was registered as her new master. But Bibby's name did appear on *Caroline*'s re-registration certificate when she was sold to new owners on the island of

The silver medal commemorating the loss of the East Indiaman *Kent*, 1825, by Thomas Halliday. (*NMM MEC2131*)

Dominica on May 10, 1827.[53] The reason for that may only be that his name had been transferred from the earlier certificate. The *Caroline* was re-registered yet again on February 27, 1829, at which time she had been cut down to a deck and a half. She then disappears from history.[54]

The only later history linked to the *Caroline*'s part in the drama is a last and very ordinary human tragedy in Liverpool. After making his second distribution of the company's gratuity, the company's agent at Liverpool, James Milligan, died. The sum due to the carpenter, and to five of the seamen, remained to his account, and had to be transferred to his successor. It is probable that the seamen had been shanghaied into other ships, perhaps after a night of celebration with the money they received in the first distribution, or when they were paid on April 16th.[55]

The part Robert Bibby and the *Caroline*'s crew played in the rescue was not recognized on the *Kent* medal, but it appears that he continued to play an active role in the commercial and shipping life of Liverpool. *Lloyd's List* for 1830 shows a 299-ton ship called the *Mary Bibby*, built in 1825, registered in Liverpool, and owned by Bibby & Co., but commanded by Captain Whitburne. The *Times* reported that a Liverpool merchant by the name of Robert Bibby was paid a dividend in April 1830. In the subsequent decade there is frequent mention of arrivals in Liverpool of the *Mary Bibby*, from Hamburg, Rio, and south Asian ports, but a report in the *Times* in 1835 of a different ship belonging to J. Bibby & Co. being fired on from the fortress at Tariffa, Spain, suggests that if Robert were proprietor, he was not the principal owner.[56] Companies House has no record of a Bibby & Co.[57] In the 1841 census, Robert is described as a merchant living at Riverview Road in the Seacombe district of Wallasey in Wirrall just across the river from Liverpool. By then his family consisted of his wife Elizabeth and two daughters, Ellen aged ten and Elizabeth, aged six. In 1851, Robert was living on Brougham Road, Wallasey, a few yards from his old home, and was described in the census as a rope maker, which is a career that a sea captain might reasonably adopt in later life. At that time his older daughter was away from home, but he was employing two servants.[58] There was more than one Robert Bibby in Cheshire and Lancaster at that time, and none died in Wirrall or Liverpool.[59]

On March 8th, the Board of the Anglo–Mexican Association met at 7 St. Helen's Place, Bishopgate Street, in London and passed a resolution "recognizing the merit of Captain Cook" and the members of the Association. It did not immediately vote any funds itself, but ordered the association's correspondence secretary, William Merry, to communicate with the East India Company and the secretary at war urging "that Captain Cook's conduct may receive such consideration as it may seem to merit." The letter to the war department was sent with a covering note from Joseph Lowe who was the association's secretary, and the war department obtained advice from the Navy Board, which was responsible for the material organization of the Royal Navy. William Morton, who was First Chief Clerk of the Navy Board, suggested that payments be made to Captain Cook of £150, with £50 for the first mate, £30 for the acting second mate, £10 each for what was thought to be the nine men of the crew, and £10 each for the 26 miners. After its receipt on March 30th, the letter was minuted "grant what is recommended."[60]

The Association was not to prove a long-term success, partly because of frauds that depressed the London stock market and prevented the new mining companies obtaining their full capitalization, and partly because the cost of transporting steam engines to the mines and supplying them with fuel greatly reduced their value. Some of the new mining companies quickly went out of business, but some companies, such as the Anglo–Mexican Association, had committed themselves to Mexican interests for a stipulated period of years. On May 31, 1825, Anglo–Mexican Mining had concluded a contract with the government of the state of Guanajuato to mint silver coin, after which the Association was divided into an Anglo–Mexican Mint Association, and an Anglo–Mexican Mining Association. This proved to be a mixed blessing. Despite the mint contract, which was later described as being injurious to that government's revenue, cash flow was less than had been anticipated. Lowe advertised in the *Times* on December 3, 1825, that a call was being made on all subscribers for £5 a share to increase the working capital.[61] In the summer of 1826 there was speculation in London that the Association had come to grief, but for the moment that was found to be an exaggeration.[62] The subscribers held a meeting on September 6, 1826, under the chairmanship of David Barclay M.P., the banker, and another on January 4, 1827.[63] The venture was described in the *Times* as a "bubble," a fraudulent scheme, and in October, the £100 shares were selling for a discounted £48. "G.H." considered that "What number of the above shares were appropriated to the directors, what number they may have sold, and what profits they may have realized, amidst this wreck of property, it is incumbent upon the directors to show."[64]

There was reported to have been a very large turnout at the January meeting, but Barclay was able to send the investors away satisfied. "The amount of silver coined up to the 16th of September last was 322,390 dollars exclusive of the ores remaining on hand, and bars of silver, containing a portion of gold, sent to the mint in Mexico to be coined. This produce was independent of the ores sold at the weekly sales in the cases where they were raised by the Buscones [Mexican entrepreneurs]." Whether the amount was in Mexican pesos or American dollars was not made clear. Less satisfactory was the advice that "an improved method of smelting had not as yet been brought to a satisfactory result." But Barclay expressed his opinion that the Association was so soundly based, that it was reasonable for it to apply for a Royal Charter. On May 6, 1834, the Proprietors met to discuss the prospects of paying a dividend, and it was agreed to pay twelve shillings.[65] Holders of certificates were asked to leave them at the Association office for two days for payment, and the issuance of new certificates.

On April 23, 1842, the contract with Guanajuato to mint coin was extended for 14 years, and on December 23, 1842, the Mint Association concluded a contract with the state of Zacatecas. But times had changed, and Mexican regulators ruled that the sovereign right for Zacatecas to mint coin could not be privatized. The *Times* speculated that the Guanajuato contract was open to the same objection.[66] The price of a £100 share in the Mining Association was only £1-3/4 on the first of November.[67] The outbreak of war between the United States and Mexico on April 25, 1846, did not favor business. Although a peace was concluded on February 2, 1848, the *Times* noted two months later that mining operations were badly affected.[68] By that time it had also become apparent that the Cornish miners, skilled as they were, lacked the theoretical geology needed to apply their experience as tin miners in Cornwall to mining other metals in places with entirely different structures.

The Mexican government renewed the mint contract for another ten years in 1853 in return for $300,000, which was reportedly used to purchase arms in Europe.[69] But it was noticed in a letter to the *Times* that J. D. Powles, who was secretary of the London Dock Company and was proceeding to Paris as part of a British delegation to Emperor Napoleon III, might also consider himself "the self-elected representative of the ruined shareholders of the Anglo–Mexican Mining Association, of the Zacatacas Company, of the Colombia Mining Association, of the New Granada Company of 1834, and of the Mines Gerres Company, he having been a promoter of and an active director in the whole of these defunct speculations." Ominously, that was not all. "He might also be considered as a self-constituted representative of the St. John Dal Rey Company, the Mexican and South American Company, the Anglo–Mexican Mint Company, the English and Australian Copper Company, the Port Philip Company, the Mariquita Company, and the Magdalena Steam Company, for he has, at the present moment, a seat in the respective directions of these companies."[70] All the same, in April 1858, the Anglo–Mexican Association was able to pay investors a dividend of 16 shillings and sixpence, and a year later, a dividend of one pound 12 shillings.[71]

But if the fortunes of the Anglo–Mexican Association were less than the dreams of Avarice, the Cornish miners and their families were so strongly established in Mexico that to this day their descendants are a part of its cultural mosaic. The city of Pachuca retains vestiges of its Cornish inheritance, including the facade of the Real del Monte Company Office, a Methodist Church built by the miners, a town clock chiming like London's Big Ben, a "Cornish" cemetery, and four Cornish Engine Houses at Mina Acosta, Mina San Pedro, Mina Delores, and Mina Corteza. Cornish pasties, modified to suit Mexican tastes, can be purchased.

LIKE Colonel Fearon, Duncan MacGregor did not sail to India in the *Charles Grant* or the *Lord Hungerford*. He went on half pay on March 26, 1825, and took his family home to Scotland for a rest. Joanna confessed that "for some weeks I was unable to write, and for part of the time even to read letters or anything to agitate the mind." She was bled twice, carefully nursed, and gradually recovered. Baby John also had a period of dangerous illness, but recovered. With understandable prejudice Elizabeth asserted that "a more engaging, lovely child, never blessed a mother's arms."

It was in Edinburgh that MacGregor found a publisher for his narrative. In the course of the next 72 years it was reprinted in Glasgow, in Dublin where it was taken up first by the Society for Promoting the United and Scriptural Education, and then in London in 1834 by the Society for Promoting Christian Knowledge, and in 1859 by the Religious Tract Society.[72] An American trade publisher in Boston, Perkins and Marvin, published an edition in 1830, followed by one in New York by Saxton and Miles in 1842, and later, in Philadelphia, by the Baptist General

Tract Society. A German translation was published in Hamburg and in 1861 an Italian one in Turin. It is not known whether the later emendations that were made to the text were MacGregor's work, or that of the editors and reflect the evangelical purpose to which it was put.

As though they had not suffered enough, the family experienced another terrible storm at sea on their way back south to London, and were only saved from destruction by a fortunate improvement in the weather. MacGregor's qualities were recognized at the Horse Guards and he was promoted to Lieutenant Colonel in the 93rd, the Sutherland Highlanders. In that capacity he served in the garrisons in Barbados, Antigua, St. Lucia, Dominica, and back to Barbados. But he had to go alone because Elizabeth was delivered of another baby and no one wanted them to risk their health in the West Indies, let alone commit them to another ocean voyage.

By an amazing quirk of fate, MacGregor was in Barbados when, on Saturday, September 30, 1826, the bottle containing the letter he had written his father from the burning wreck of the *Kent* was found. According to a local newspaper, it was seen on the white beach at Bathsheba in the Parish of St. Joseph on the rugged east side of Barbados, "by a gentleman who was bathing there, who, on breaking it, found the melancholy account of the fate of the ship *Kent*, contained in a folded paper, written with pencil, but scarcely legible."[73] MacGregor returned to England in 1828 and then served in Canterbury, Weedon in Northamptonshire, and Ireland.[74]

MacGregor was a leader in the establishment of a regimental school. He told his sister in 1828 that he informed "the regiment that I had two distinct objects in view. First, that I might see fulfilled in the 93rd Highlanders the pious wish expressed by our late Sovereign respecting his people at large that they should not only possess Bibles, but that every man should be able to read his Bible, and second to enable young men of steadiness and honest ambition to qualify themselves for the respectable rank of non-commissioned officers."[75]

As his abilities suggest was inevitable, MacGregor was to go far in the army. He came into the public eye in 1836 when he gave evidence to the commission struck to consider the efficacy of corporal punishment in the army. His conviction was that it was not often appropriate, at least not in a regiment such as the Sutherlands raised in a close-knit community where everyone was known.[76] In December 1837, the regiment was concentrated at Cork before sailing in two divisions for Halifax in Nova Scotia to deal with the threat of rebellion in the colonies of Upper and Lower Canada. The weather was so bad that MacGregor's division did not reach port until March 5, 1838, the third time he and his family had to face the worst that the sea could offer. An account of him at this time says that "when the 93rd was in Halifax Nova Scotia every one of the soldiers used to march to church with his Bible and Presbyterian Psalm-book under his arm, and it is on record on one occasion nearly 700 of them partook in the sacrament."[77] An old soldier who was once asked how he liked being under MacGregor's command replied, "He was just the richt officer to command oor regiment. He was strict eneuch to us sojers but just forebye. He whiles spoke to us in the Gaelic, of oorselves and oor families and helped mony a man after he left the corps. He was an upright and religious man and we shall, I doubt, not see his like again in the auld 'Rories.'" Rories was a nickname for the private soldier in the 93rd.[78]

MacGregor returned home at the end of the year and, from 1838 to October 19, 1858, spent 20 years as Inspector General of the Police Service of Northern Ireland.[79] There is a family story that

Daniel O'Connell, the Irish nationalist and human rights campaigner, took an opportunity to shake MacGregor by the hand and thank him, saying that "he had always acted with great consideration and perfect fairness towards his countrymen."[80] He was knighted a Commander of the Bath in the civil division on December 26, 1848, and reached the rank of Major General in 1851.[81]

In 1854, MacGregor was to be in the public eye again when he testified against a plan to use the Irish constabulary to collect the excise tax.[82] In 1857, he was promoted to Lieutenant General, but his wife Elizabeth died in March 1858 at Drumcondra Castle near Dublin.[83] At the time of the 1861 census he was a widower, living at 24 Norfolk Crescent, Paddington, with his son, a 29-year-old daughter Elizabeth Joanna Anne, a cook, a nurse, a lady's maid, and a footman.[84] He was promoted to the brevet rank of General in 1864 and confirmed in rank in 1877.[85] At the time of the 1881 census, the last year of his life and just a few weeks after his 94th birthday, MacGregor was living at 2 Vanburgh Park, Greenwich, in Kent with his daughter Elizabeth now married to Lieutenant Colonel Robert W. Brooke. The family was completed by his two grandsons, Graham W., age 16, and Eardly W., age 11. There were also five servants.[86] His son John reported that MacGregor "had always and often told me, when speaking of his end, that although he did not wish to dictate to God how he should die, yet, if it were His will, he prayed that it might be sudden, without any death-bed scenes, and that he might be ever kept in a state to meet Him." This last wish was granted, and "his was not a death but a sudden translation from death to life. I was with him twenty minutes before his departure, and the last to clasp his hand or speak to him."[87]

John MacGregor was to become a popular figure. He accompanied his father to Halifax in 1838, shared his muscular Christianity, and in 1856 while participating in a prayer meeting at Lanark race course, met the sailor who had handed him up the side of the *Cambria* 31 years before.[88] He worked as a barrister in London, and after a railway accident forced him to abandon marksmanship, he designed the first European sailing canoe. Fifteen feet long, 28 inches wide, nine inches deep and weighing 80 pounds (36 kg), it was double-ended like Indian canoes, but built with lapstrake oak planking, and decked in cedar covered with rubberized canvas with an open cockpit in the center. He named the canoe *Rob Roy* after his distinguished outlaw ancestor, and his own nickname. Using its sail and a double-bladed paddle, MacGregor voyaged extensively in the Baltic and the Middle East. In 1866, he founded the English Royal Canoe Club and published *A Thousand Miles in the Rob Roy Canoe*, which made him a small fortune and introduced the middle class to this new way of enjoying nature. An accomplished artist, he drew all the illustrations in his books.

AFTER being told of his KCB, Colonel Fearon's movements during the remainder of the year 1825 are not known. A Mr. Fearon attended Francis Burdett's Westminster election dinner on May 24th and demonstrated his loyalty to the crown by "a solitary hiss (laughter)." But there was a wine merchant and a carpet dealer with the same name in London at the time, so this is scant evidence.[89] On January 12, 1826, however, it is known that Colonel Fearon exchanged into the 64th Regiment, and on December 14, 1827 he was voted a Freeman of the City of Cork, "to mark the estimation in which this council holds his humane and intrepid conduct on the occasion of the burning of the *Kent*." This honor he accepted very gracefully, replying that it had been his "good fortune to be associated in that afflicting event with a Class of Individuals, each of whom manifested a high degree of heroism and self-devotion, and therefore left but little to be done by him whom chance more than merit placed at their head."[90] Some time after that he and his family continued on their way to India. He exchanged again into the 6th, was promoted to full Colonel on June 20, 1829, and served as Deputy Adjutant-General of the Madras garrison.[91] There, at St. George's church on November 2, 1830, his eldest daughter, Margaret-Eliza Fearon, was to be married to the Honorable Sir Ralph Palmer, Chief Justice of the Supreme Court of Judicature of the Madras Presidency.[92] Thus her married name became the same as her stepmother's maiden name. It is told that Sir Ralph read an account of the *Kent* disaster and promptly decided that a girl who could lead the regimental women to safety over the high stern of an Indiaman was the one he wanted to marry.[93]

In November 1838, Colonel Fearon exchanged into the 40th Regiment of Foot, and on February 14th following, it was announced that he was to assume command at Poonah.[94] But his life was not to end happily. His wife Mary gave birth to two more children, Letitia Halkett born August 24, 1827, and Georgina Augusta born exactly two years later, but some time after that she returned to England, where Letitia died in Devonport February 3, 1832. Mary later left town suddenly without paying several accounts. She owed £158/3/2 for clothing to a Richard King, who wrote her husband on January 20, 1834, and on February 25, 1835, a trades woman of Devonport protesting at his refusal to pay, "unless compelled to by law. . . I believe your letter went on to say that a man is not bound to pay for the extravagance of his wife but most assuredly if a man can send a wife home from abroad whom he knew to be extravagant and whose husband is known, as you Sir are, to hold a lucrative situation under our Government to the payment of which we all contribute . . ." etc. Evidently she found the

Colonel unsympathetic, possibly because he was financially embarrassed beyond his means. He was promoted Major General on November 9, 1846, but it appears he may have retired in 1844 due to ill health, and that he died at the home of his daughter, Lady Palmer, at Much Hadham, Hertfordshire, on January 24, 1851. Colburn's *United Service Magazine* reported that the cause of death was suicide. Four boxes of closely-written legal documents found their way into the archives of the India Office. Among them is a letter from R. B. Bennett dated March 25, 1836, asking payment for the education provided Fearon's son, and which was annotated on August 7, 1855, by R.B.S. that the account was to be left "with the rest to be settled in such way as Messrs. Bowers and Willis or yourself shall consider equitable and just."[95]

Dr. Townsend told his sister that he had only a single sovereign saved, but that he would "make the best of my way to London as well as I can." He arrived there at the house of a Mr. Morgans, 11 Chenies Street, by March 9th when he wrote his family to say that he was going "to the India House to see if they will give me any allowance & send me out free of expenses—if they do not I do not know what will become of me. I have lost, I am sure, upwards of five hundred pounds." He had hope of recovering from Coutts bank a letter of credit for £40 lost in the wreck.[96] Whatever role he may have had in the Falmouth narrative, he did not have any financial resources to pay for its printing, which was done "by and for" James Philip, a Falmouth bookseller, and dedicated by "the Publisher" on 16 March.[97] Townsend may have traveled with Captain Cook; the Reverend Frederick Trestrail later recalled that he had been with Townsend as far as Plymouth.[98] Whether or not it was because the company refused to pay his fare on another ship going to India or that he lost interest, Townsend tendered his resignation to the court on April 12, 1826, and returned to Cork. where he was employed by the work house. He later entered into private practice.[99] He appears to have lived the rest of his life in Cork, or Queenstown as it was known from the time of Queen Victoria's visit in 1848 to 1922 after Irish independence. It is attractive to wonder whether he met MacGregor in December 1837 when the latter was embarking at Cork for Halifax.

If the Reverend Trestrail's memory is to be relied on, Townsend did meet another friend from that hard experience. In the autobiography that Trestrail's wife edited after his death, he wrote that in 1840 he took up an appointment at Cork and went to call:

When I entered his consulting room he received me with great cordiality, but was much moved and silently pointed to a large engraving on the wall, of the burning of the *Kent*. In a few moments he recovered his composure and sent for Mrs. Townsend, and a very tall, elegant lady entered and greeted me with a warmth that exceeded anything I had before met with. I felt at home at once, and in all my subsequent intercourse with the family this cordiality increased. I found Dr. Townsend's social position was a high one. His brother, Horace, was High Sheriff of the county, his sister a highly cultivated lady, and the Recorder of the city and other professional gentlemen made up a circle of intelligent and cultivated friends. To all these the doctor introduced me as "the friend who had succoured him in his distress."

In July 1857, Dr. Townsend was awarded with the degree of Bachelor of Laws, apparently at Dublin.[100] On May 12th of the following year, he was admitted a Member of the Royal College of Surgeons.[101] His obituary is dated January 6, 1878. He was aged 78 when he died, and was an honorary Fellow of the King and Queen's College of Physicians. His obituarist wrote that "in his personal relations, as well as in his professional capacity, he was widely respected. He was a man of general culture as well as of ability in his own particular calling, and when, on the death of the late Archdeacon O'Shea, he was called upon to assume the office of President of the Cork Library, the fitness of the choice was generally approved."[102]

A little is also known about some other survivors. Dr. Busteed, who presented his copy of MacGregor's narrative to the India Office Library, noted in the flyleaf that he had known Dr. Townsend well from 1849 to 1855. He also noted that he was "almost" certain that Colonel Fearon's daughter Frederica Eliza married Mr. (later Sir) Alexander John Arbuthnot.[103] Both had been three years old when the *Kent* burned in 1825. Arbuthnot did not travel out to India as a writer in the East India Company until 1842, and his marriage took place on 1 February 1844. A colonel's daughter, even if a little past the usual age for women to marry, would have been advantageous for a poor boy whose widowed mother had started him out in life by moving to Rugby where he could study under the iconic teacher Dr. Thomas Arnold as a day boy. In March 1855, following the suppression of the Indian Mutiny and of the East India Company, Arbuthnot was appointed as the first director of the newly formed department of public instruction in the government of India, and went on to found Madras and Calcutta universities, both of which he served as Vice-Chancellor. In

1875, he was appointed to the Governor General's Council. He took an active part in dealing with the south Indian famine of 1877–78, and in 1879 strenuously opposed Sir Louis Cavagnari's expedition to Kabul with a small escort and the subsequent aggressive policy toward Afghanistan.[104] His wife died in 1898, 63 years after the loss of the *Kent*.

Another obituary pasted into Dr. Busteed's copy was that of the *Kent*'s purser, William E. Browne, who died at the age of 79 at Freemantle, in Hampshire near Southampton. He was credited with "regardless of all personal risks, exerting himself heroically in saving the women and children from the wreck." Eight years later, in 1833, Browne had again suffered shipwreck in the Honorable East India Company ship the *Duke of York* when he again lost all his personal property. In December 1825, only nine months after the disastrous end of the *Kent*, the first steam-assisted ship, the *Enterprise*, had made the passage from Falmouth to Calcutta.[105] It was to take some time for steam technology to displace sail in the eastern trades, but in 1845, Browne transferred to the steamer service of the Peninsular and Oriental Company which enjoyed an Admiralty mail contract to Alexandria, Egypt.[106] Life in the P&O steamers was less wearing than was that in the East India Company ships, and Browne remained with P&O until he retired in 1864.

Loss of the Kent, scrimshaw on a whale tooth by an unknown artist.

10

A Story for the Ages

THE STORY OF THE LOSS OF THE *Kent* stands out as an example of a disciplined response to crisis at sea. The survival of most of the *Kent*'s passengers and crew can be contrasted with some other nineteenth-century shipwrecks when panic prevailed and no care was taken to help the weak. When the *Northfleet* was rammed and sank in 1873, a survivor noted "there was a terrible panic among the strong, rough men, when it became apparent that the vessel was sinking. The wild rush for the boats, and the mad confusion which took place, were like the trampling of a herd of buffaloes. . . . Poor Captain Knowles, brave as a hero all this time, was nevertheless angered at the reckless selfishness of the men, and he drew a pistol and threatened the big fellows, who were leaping helter-skelter into the boats. He said, 'The boats are not for such as you; they are for the women and children.' Despite the threats and entreaties of the captain and boatswain, the men continued to throng into the boats. Captain Knowles discharged his pistol several times and wounded one man, who, however, kept his place in the boat." The *Northfleet* was an immigrant ship carrying some 400 people, and sank in a few minutes. She was anchored in the lee of Dungeness, close to land, but the ship that ran into her fled to avoid responsibility, without attempting to rescue anyone. Another ship passed by ignoring the shouts of the people in the water, and only 86 were saved when the pilot boat responded to the rockets Captain Knowles had fired.[1]

A year later, the *Cospatrick*, another immigrant ship, caught fire in the southern ocean. The Reverend Edward Hoare summed up that disaster in a collection of such accounts as *Perils of the Deep*. "It would not be easy to imagine a sadder tale of 'sea-sorrow.' . . . There is absolutely nothing to relieve the lurid light and dark shadows that hang over the scene. Scarce any element of horror is absent—enormous loss of life, terrible confusion, wild despair, hunger, thirst, madness, cannibalism—in a word, but three survivors to tell the story of how four hundred and seventy of their fellows perished miserably!"[2]

The experience of the *Kent* differed from the story of many other disasters because there was hope that all the passengers and crew of the *Kent* could be transferred to the *Cambria*, despite the terrific sea, if everyone acted in a disciplined way. When ships foundered out of sight of help and the only hope lay in finding space in a lifeboat, baser instincts were given stronger play. Another important factor in the story of the *Kent* was that its passengers were almost all from a crack infantry regiment with recent battle experience. A force that could form a square in the face of a cavalry charge had the capacity to maintain discipline in a shipwreck, even though it was out of its element. And it is possible that the evangelical Christianity of some of the regiment strengthened their sense of duty. Charles Dickens introduced his account of the disaster by quoting one of Dr. Arnold's sermons in which he asserted that, "Never was the faith and charity of martyrs shown more beautifully than in the Christian soldiers and sailors so nobly united amid the horrors of that scene in the service of God."[3]

MacGregor was not primarily concerned with survival: "None of those soldiers who are in the habit of reading their Bibles can have failed to notice, that faith in Jesus Christ, the Son of God, is therein made the great pivot on which the salvation of man hinges; that the whole human race, without distinction of rank, nation, age, or sex, being justly exposed to the wrath of Almighty God, nothing but the precious blood of Christ which was shed on the cross can possibly atone for their sins; and that faith in this atonement can alone pacify the conscience, and awaken confidence towards God as a reconciled Father."[4] MacGregor's personal theology was a generous one. He cautioned his readers not to forget that "the religion of the Bible is a religion of motives, rather than one of observances," and warned that those who follow the law without the substance are spiritually dead. But at the same time he warned against sliding away from the law of God, only to find at the hour of death "that the sand which he had all his lifetime been mistaking for the 'Rock of ages,' is now giving way under his feet." Repentance must come before death.

As a soldier, MacGregor felt that soldiers had a particular need to be on their spiritual guard, and only to be content when they feel the work of grace expressed in their life and conversation.

> He will be zealous and steady in the performance of duty, patient under fatigue and privation, sober amid temptations, calm but firm in the hour of danger, and respectfully obedient to his officers; he will honor his king, be content with his wages, and do harm to no man. His piety will be ardent but sober; his prayers

will be earnest and frequent, but rather in secret than before men; he will not be contentious or disputatious, but rather desirous of instructing others by his example than by his precepts; making his light so to shine before them, in the simplicity of his motives, the uprightness of his actions, in his readiness to oblige, and by the whole tenor of his life, that they seeing his good works, may be led, by the Divine blessing, to acknowledge the reality, and power, and beauty of religion, and be induced in like manner to glorify his heavenly Father. In short, in comparison with his thoughtless comrades, he must not only aspire to become a better man, but, from the constraining motives of the Gospel, struggle to be also in every essential respect a better soldier.

In conclusion, I would observe, that if any class of men, more than another, ought to be struck with awe and gratitude by the goodness and providence of God, it is they who go down to the sea in ships, and see his wonders in the great deep, or if any ought to familiarize their minds with death, and its solemn consequences, it is surely soldiers, "whose very business it is to die."

His solemn conclusion from the awful experiences on the *Kent* and in the rescue was that at any time "the message may come forth, as it lately did, at an hour when it is least expected, 'This night thy soul is required of thee!'" It is evident, however, that the spiritual armor MacGregor described, valuable in its own right in a religious sense, is also the strongest possible preparation for meeting such disasters as the fire and storm that overcame the *Kent*. MacGregor's Christianity had a strong practical element which insured that faith did not lead to fatalism.

THE paintings made by William Daniell, Thomas Buttersworth, Joseph Kronheim, and Thomas Hemy all support a heroic interpretation of the events surrounding the destruction of the *Kent*, and in doing so they stand in stark contrast with the famous painting by the French artist Théodore Géricault, who in 1819 exhibited in Paris his *Raft of the Medusa*, the subject of which was the abandonment at sea by their officers of a raft crowded with shipwrecked soldiers. The *Medusa* was a French frigate serving as a troop transport which struck the Bank of Arguin off the coast of Mauritania in 1816. Géricault's object was to suggest that the restored monarchy of Louis XVIII had as little concern for the welfare of the French population as the French army officers had had for their men. In 1820, Géricault had brought the picture to London where its great commercial success suggests that the British public were no less interested in the theme.[5] MacGregor may have had that in mind as he wrote his narrative about a very different experience, in which the officers did not desert their men, and strongly suggested the importance of religion in that outcome.

It needs to be asked why in writing his narrative MacGregor minimized the facts he told his father about how the first boat to be launched, the gig, was rushed by panicky men who took the places intended for the women, overset the boat, and were drowned. The suppression of this part of the story was clearly deliberate, but it should not be assumed that it was intended as myth building about the heroism of the 31st Regiment. When the Reverend Edward Hoare's account of the *Northfleet* and *Cospatrick* disasters was published in 1885 by the Society for Promoting Christian Knowledge, a connection between religion and right behavior was not made explicit. The purpose of that society, and of the others which kept MacGregor's narrative in print for so many years, was more to remind readers of the transience of life, and of the importance of faith in things eternal.

To the modern mind, the idea that the role of men is to protect women and children, who should be given first place in the lifeboats because of their physical and spiritual nature, undermines women's autonomy and power. MacGregor's was a religion of sacrifice, which understood that it might be appropriate for men to die so that women could live, while at the same time understanding that women's roles also involved sacrifice; life was a partnership and the ultimate good was a heavenly one. These are big questions, but that MacGregor and his generation were not entirely wrong is manifestly evident by the outcome of the story of the *Kent*.

Undoubtedly, MacGregor's main motive in minimizing the panic of a few was one of charity toward those who had died, and toward their families. Recounting how some of them had acted selfishly, and died as a result, would have put a shadow on the memories of all who died. As MacGregor said, he had seen that some who behaved badly at first later found an inner strength that enabled them to overcome their fears, while others lost their courage as they became exhausted. Even the much criticized men of the *Kent*'s cutter crew, after their panicked attempt to get onboard the *Cambria*, turned to and made repeated crossings of the stormy sea throughout the day to rescue survivors. The tragedy of the *Kent* showed more of courage and generous humanity by the officers and men of the ships and the regiment, and by their families, than it did of human weakness.

Glossary

aft, abaft. At, in, or towards the stern of a vessel.

beam on. To the side of a ship or boat.

brace aback. To bring the wind onto the forward side of the sails to slow the ship.

broach. To cause to veer broadside to the wind and waves; also, to make a hole in.

bulwark. The part of a ship's side above the upper deck.

carvel planking. A hull made with flush or edge to edge planks rather than overlapping.

chains, chain plates. The plate or bar by which the standing rigging is attached to the hull.

channel. The ledge projecting from a sailing ship's sides to spread the shrouds and keep them clear of the gunnels.

close-hauled. With sails trimmed flat for sailing as close to the wind as possible.

coamings. A raised rim around an opening, as on a deck, designed to keep water out.

crowd. To spread a large amount of sail to increase speed.

deadlight. A strong shutter placed over a porthole or cabin window in stormy weather.

falls. The rope tackle used to hoist a lifeboat.

following sea. An overtaking sea that comes from the stern.

gallery, galleries. The platform or balcony at the stern, often enclosed and containing accommodations.

gunnel; also, *gunwale.* The upper edge of a ship's side.

hard-a-lee. The command to move the tiller leeward to tack the ship.

helm. The steering apparatus.

hove to. To bring or come to a stop by backing some but not all of the sails.

jib. A triangular sail from the foretopmast to a boom or bowsprit at the bow.

lade. To load with cargo.

laying to a painter. To secure a boat by a rope to its bow.

leeward. Situated on or moving toward the side away from which the wind is blowing.

mainsail. The principal sail of a vessel.

poop. The stern superstructure of a ship.

reef, reefed. To shorten or reduce the size of a sail exposed to the wind by taking it in, usually by rolling and securing it with ties; a sail so shortened.

rove. To fasten by passing a rope or line through a hole or block.

scuttle. A small opening or hatch in the deck or hull of a ship.

spanker boom. The boom to which the spanker sail located abaft the after mast is attached.

stay. A heavy rope used to brace or support a mast or yard.

staysail. A triangular sail hoisted on a stay.

stern. The rear part of a ship.

tack. To bring a ship into the wind in order to change the direction or course of a vessel.

tiller ropes. Ropes attached to the tiller used as a lever to turn the rudder of a ship.

topgallant sail. The sail above the topsail.

topsail. A sail set above the lowest sail on a mast.

trim. The fore and aft balance of a ship.

tumblehome. The narrowing a ship's beam from the waterline to the above decks.

windward. Of or on the side exposed to the wind.

yard. A spar hung at right angles to the mast on which the sail is attached and spread.

Notes

ABBREVIATIONS USED IN REFERENCES:

BL/IOR   British Library, India Office Records.
ESRJ   *East Surrey Regiment Journal*
MUN   Memorial University of Newfoundland
NA/PRO   National Archives, Public Records Office
NMM   National Maritime Museum
SHC   Surrey History Centre
WBCA   *West Briton and Cornwall Advertiser*

PREFACE: A LETTER FROM A FRIEND

1. Susan Darwin to Charles Darwin, January 3, 1826, *The Correspondence of Charles Darwin*, Vol. 1, p. 25.
2. Charles Dickens, *All Year Round*, November 24, 1866, p. 444.
3. Edwin Hodder, *John MacGregor (Rob Roy)*, London: Hodder Brothers, 1894.
4. Townsend transcripts made by C. E. C. Townsend, March 1988. See also Dr. Townsend's letter, *ESRJ*, August 1927, Vol. 2 no. 33, p. 2. The dates on the transcript are March 4, 10, and 11, the last being published in the *ESRJ* as March 20. There are discrepancies between the transcripts. Bray transcript supplied by Daniel Fearon, May 28, 2008.
5. Edward William Bray to Loftus A. Bryan, 10 Bride Street, Dublin, Falmouth, March 10, 1825; transcript supplied by Daniel Feron, May 28, 2008.

6 . BL/IOR MSS Eur A59, MacGregor, *Narrative*. Obituary inside cover dated January 6, 1878. Anon. [Reverend Edgcombe Rimmell], *A Narrative of the Loss by Fire of the Honourable East [India] Company's Ship Kent on her voyage to India*, Falmouth: by and for J. Philip; and sold by J. Richardson, Royal Exchange, London, March 16, 1825. "Dedicated to Captain Cook of the Cambria, Captain Cobb, and the gallant officers of the 31 Regiment of Foot." A "second edition" was advertised in the *WBCA* on April, 1 1825. Edgcombe Rimmell was born in 1803, the son of Robert Rimmell of Falmouth, and was curate of Mabe near Falmouth in 1831, of Penzance in 1834, and of St. Blazey in 1839. A harvest sermon that he wrote and had printed in 1840 at Launceston refers back to his being the author of the 1825 narrative. George Clement Boase and William Prideaux Courtney, *Bibliotheca Cornubiensis. A catalogue of the writings . . . of Cornishmen, and of works relating to the county of Cornwall, etc.* 3 vols., London: Longmans & Co., 1874–82; vol. 2 (1878), pp. 571–2.

7. Thomas Buttersworth, *The Loss of the East Indiaman Kent in the Bay of Biscay*, March 1, 1825, BHC3819 8 National Maritime Museum, London.

8. When he enlisted in the navy on August 17, 1795 at the age of 27, he must already have been a professional sailor because he was rated an able seaman. On November 26, 1796, he was rated a master-at-arms, and on March 1, 1800, he was promoted to midshipman, but he was then invalided home from Minorca effective the 7th of May. There is some mystery about this, because *Caroline* was not at Minorca on that date, and Buttersworth's name does not appear on the Minorca hospital muster list. That he was actually on board *Caroline* for at least part of the period is suggested by his bill with Sam Nicholson the purser for tobacco, but his "medical" discharge might just possibly have been a cover for something more interesting. *Caroline's* Pay Book, NA/PRO ADM 35/316: 3; Captain's Logs ADM 51/1261 and 1381; and Port Mahon Hospital Records, ADM 102/706 and 707.

9. In 1784, his uncle, Thomas Daniell, was the first British artist to obtain permission from the East India Company to travel to India, and he took his fifteen-year-old nephew with him.

10. London: Longman, Hurst, Rees & Orme, 1810. In 1823, William Daniell returned to the subject painting, *An East Indiaman in a gale off the Cape of Good Hope*.

11. January 1825.

12. William Daniell [artist, engraver & publisher], *Kent Indiaman on Fire, in the Bay of Biscay*, BM 1917.12.8.2732; *The Cambria brig, receiving on board the last boatload, from the Kent Indiaman on fire*, December 6, 1825, aquatint, tinted, 375mm x 518mm, National Maritime Museum PAH0543.

13. BL/IOR, L/MAR/B 41 I, *Kent* Journal to March 29, 1824, second voyage.

14. John Brinkel collection, manufactured by "Church Army" of 14 Edgware Rd. W.2., London, England. Hand colored. Thomas Hemy was born at Castel, Jersey, Channel Islands in 1851(?), one of thirteen children, ten boys and three girls, and had at least two artist brothers—Charles Napier Hemy of Newcastle, England (1841–1917) and Bernard Benedict Hemy (1844–1910). Obituary: *Times*, April 7, 1937; pg. 18; Issue 47652; col B.

15 Lieutenant Warneford, R.N., pseud. [William Russell], *The Jolly Boat; or, Perils and Disasters Illustrating Courage, Endurance, and Heroism in the Merchang-Marine Service*, London: John Maxwell and Co., 1865, p. 184. Some of the many abstractions are included in the bibliography.

16. James Hedderwick, *The English Orator*, 1833, p. 45.

CHAPTER 1: FITTING OUT

1. Allan Speedy, Ed., *Mrs Livingstone I presume, Memoirs of Sarah Speedy, Waterloo to Waikato*, http://www.speedy.co.nz/recollections/

2. *Times*, August 3, 1820; pg. 2, Issue 11002, col G; August 11, 1820, pg. 3, Issue 11009, col G; November 14, 1822, pg. 2, Issue 11716, col B; December 28, 1822, pg. 2, Issue 11754, col C; January 7, 1823, pg. 2, Issue 11762, col G; .

3. Jean Sutton, *Lords of the East, the East India Company and its Ships*, London: Conway Maritime Press, 1981, p. 36; 39 Geo III, Chapter 89. In a consolidating act of June 5, 1818, 58 George III, Chapter 83, it was laid down that when the East India Company wanted to hire a ship for its regular trade it was to advertise for tenders, and specify the dimensions of the ship it wanted, and the freights it was willing to pay.

4. NA/PRO CUST 130/3 # 287, *Kent*. BT 107/34 # 25, *Kent* The figures given in Rowan Hackman, *Ships of the East India Company*, 2001, are evidently wrong.

5. NA/PRO CUST 130/3 # 287, *Kent*.

6. NA/PRO BT 107/34 # 25, *Kent*.

7. Anthony Farrington, *Catalogue of East India Company Ships Journals and Logs, 1600–1834*, London: British Library, 1999.

8. BL/IOR Catalogue, *Kent*: Voyages: (1) 1820/1 Bombay and China. Capt Henry Cobb. Cowes March 14, 1821—June 10 Bombay—August 29 Singapore—Sept. 24 Whampoa—December 29 Second Bar—May 2, 1822 St. Helena—June 27 Downs. (2) 1822/3 Bengal and China. Capt Henry Cobb. Downs January 7, 1823—May 9, New Anchorage—August 1 Penang—August 21 Singapore—September 30 Whampoa—November 16 Second Bar—February 7, 1824 St. Helena—March 22 Downs. (3) 1824/5 Bengal and China. Capt Henry Cobb. Downs February 18, 1825—March 1 burnt in the Bay of Biscay.

9. Charles Hardy, and Horatio Charles A. Hardy, *Registry of Ships*, 4th ed., London, 1835, pp. 64–65, 111.

10. BL/IOR, MS Eur G118, Hickey, *op. cit*, v. 1 pp. 278–280; Sutton, p. 71.

11. Anthony Farrington, *A Biographical Index of East India Company Maritime Service Officers, 1600–1834*, British Library, 1999.

12. Hodder, p. 12.

13. MacGregor, Appendix 6, Letter from the Officers of the 31st Regiment, officers of the *Kent*, and Passengers, to Captain W. Cook, commanding the *Cambria* Brig, Falmouth Harbor.

14. In 1821 he was the defendant in a law suit, and was described in the *Times* report as having been a teacher of mathematics at Christ Hospital school, then a corn factor, and a ready-made cloths dealer; before studying to become a doctor of Laws, and being made a sheriff of London, and a justice of the peace. "He stood before the court at the date of the present action, a magistrate, a doctor, and a lieutenant in the navy." *Times*, December 13, 1821; pg. 3; Issue 11428; col B, "Court Of King's Bench, Westminster, Dec. 12. May V. Gwynne." *See also: Times*, May 4, 1820; pg. 2; Issue 10924; col A. *Kent's Original London Directory* of 1816 described him as a "ready-made linen warehouse," and he does not appear in the 1825 edition. His service in the Navy had begun in October 1789, under the patronage of Vice-Admiral Sir John LaForey. After service in the West Indies, and fighting in the battle of the Glorious First of June in 1794, he was commissioned Lieutenant on October 30, 1795. His naval service appears to have ended in September 1797. Little more is known about him, apart from his marriage to a Strangeways girl. He was to be put on the junior list of retired commanders in 1830 and was promoted to the senior retired list in 1836. William Richard O'Byrne, *A Naval Biographical Dictionary*, London, John Murray, 1849, vol i, p 439. Is this the Lawrence Gwynne who is shown in the 1851 census as retired to East Teignmouth? HO107; Piece: 1870; Folio: 194; Page: 20; GSU roll: 221018.

15. Commodore Dance to the Court of Directors, *Earl Camden*, August, 6, 1804, *Naval Chronicle*, Vol. 12 pp. 137–139, and Nicholas Tracy, *Naval Chronicle, Consolidated Edition*, London: Chatham Publication, 1999, vol. 3, p. 41.

16. Tracy, *Naval Chronicle, vol. 3*, p. 42.

17. BL/IOR Eur MS D1050/517. *See*: Ruth Rhynas Brown, "Guns carried on East Indiamen, 1600–1800," *International Journal of Nautical Archaeology*, February 1990—Vol. 19 Issue 1, pp. 17–22.

18. Sutton, p. 38; BL/IOR, L/MAR/1/36, 9 January 1799.

19. Joseph Farington, *The Farington Diary*, 16 vols., (eds. Garlick, Kenneth, and Macintyre, Angus—Vols 9-10 Katheryn Cave), New Haven: Yale University Press, 1979. August 7, 1806, v. 8 p. 2834. BL/IOR, MS Eur G118,

NOTES 205

Memoirs of William Hickey; Alfred Spencer ed., *Memoirs of William Hickey*, 1913, v. 4 p. 433.

20. Hardy, p. 92, 125.
21. Hardy, pp 92, 109–110.
22. BL/IOR, L/MAR/B/41S, 1824/5 Receipt Book of *Kent*.
23. Hardy, p. 86, 99, 123. See BL/IOR, L/AG/1/7/1, *Journal of Private Trade*, May 1, 1821. No breakdown is given of individual private cargoes.
24. BL/IOR, Eur MS G118, *Memoirs of William Hickey*, p. 115; Hickey, op.cit., v1, pp 248–249.
25. Hardy, pp. 92, 125.
26. Hardy, pp. 88–89.
27. Sutton, pp. 88–92.
28. *The surgeons mate: or, military and domestique surgery: discovering. . . ye method and order of ye surgeons chest, ye uses of the instruments, the vertues. . . of ye medicines, with ye. . . cures of wounds made by gunshot and otherwise:. . . a treatise of ye cure of ye plague, etc*, London: R Young for N Bourne, 2nd Edition, 1639.
29. Hickey, v 4, pp. 411–12.
30. NMM Stanfield MS 79/159 box 4.
31. *The Civil Engineer and Architect's Journal*, 1849, p. 285. *Map of Poplar*, London: Eyre and Spottiswoode, 1885.
32. Hardy, pp. 142–143.
33. NA/PRO 30/2/7/9.
34. Hardy, p. 93.
35. *The Civil Engineer and Architect's Journal*, 1849, p. 285.
36. Sutton, p. 98.
37. Allan Speedy, Ed., *Mrs Livingstone I Presume*. The flash point of turpentine is 35 degrees C, while kerosene lamp oil has a flash point of between 38 degrees and 72 degrees.
38. Hardy, p. 95.
39. Pierre Bouguer, *Traite du Navire, de sa Construction, et de ses Mouvemens*, 1746.
40. BL/IOR, L/AG/1/6/27 pp. 563–66. MacGregor, p. 7.
41. Hardy, p. 95.

CHAPTER 2: DEPARTURE

1. *Times*, December 9, 1824, pg. 2, Issue 12519, col C; and January 27, 1825; pg. 3; Issue 12561; col A.
2. BL/IOR, L/MAR/B/41S.
3. Hardy, p. 95.
4. 53 Geo. III, Chapter 155, Clause 46.

5. *Times,* January 23, 1824; pg. 2; Issue 12091; col A, "East India House, January 21, 1824," and April 1, 1824; pg. 2; Issue 12301; col *F.I. Can But it Takes Great Patience.*

6. Hardy, pp. 89–90.

7. Letter of May 23, 1803, Charles Robert Leslie. *Memoirs of the Life of John Constable.* 1843. *Reprint,* London: John Lehmann, 1949, p. 35.

8. *His Majesty's Ship Victory, Captain E. Harvey, in the Memorable Battle of Trafalgar, between two French ships of the line,* 20x28 1/2", *V&A,* WS4 169-1888. Photo CT 968. Seven of the sketches are in the Oppé collection at the *Tate Gallery,* T08120-21 and T08738-742, and another nine are in the *Victoria and Albert Museum* WD13, *vid .,* Graham Reynolds. *Catalogue of the Constable Collection.* London: HMSO, 1960, 46-9, Nos. 41–50.

9. *Times,* January 6, 1825; pg. 2; Issue 12543; col E.

10. The 2nd Battalion of the 31st Regiment had eventually become the 70th, then the Surrey Regiment in 1782, and that regiment was to be recombined with the 31st in 1881, the combined force being known as the East Surrey Regiment.

11. Michael Langley, *The East Surrey Regiment (the 31st and 70th Regiments of Foot),* London: Leo Cooper, 1972.

12. *The Annual Register, or, A View of the History and Politics of the Year. . . 1851,* p. 256. SHC, ESR 2/15/2/2, Note by Lieutenant Colonel Charles Hordern, Fearon's great-grandson. Fearon's career was mentioned in the *Gentleman's Magazine* December 1794, November 28, 1797, June 13, 1807, September 1, 1813, December 1813, and December 18, 1816. See also *Royal Military Calendar,* 1820, and S. P. Fearon, *Pedigrees of the Fearon Family Trading into China and Notes on Collateral and Other Matters of Family Interest,* private printing, n.d.

13. Hugh W. Pearse, *History of the East Surrey Regiment (31st Foot, Huntingdonshire Regiment and 70th Foot, Surrey Regiment),* London, 1916, p. 152.

14. The *Scaleby Castle* was originally built for service in eastern waters, a Country Ship, but had been brought into regular service. She made a total of fourteen voyages for the Company, and the one for 1825 was under the command of Captain David Rae Newall. Richard Cannon, *Historical record of the Thirty-first,* London: Parker, Furnivall & Parker, 1850, pp. 79–80.

15. MacGregor, p. 25.

16. Petition of Anne Currie, 25 April 1825; A Christie, Chatham, 6 May 1825, to Sir Herbert Taylor; Taylor to Joseph Dart, 23 May 1825: BL/IOR, E/1/156 ff 552–556.

17. Probable genealogy: Duncan MacGregor and Beatrix Macniven had issue: 1. John, an officer in the R.N. Commodore Bombay Marine who died at

Batavia 23 March 1784, leaving everything to his sister's son, John Paul, with the request that he take the name MacGregor. 2. Drummond Mary, married (1) Paul, whose family name had been McPhail by whom she had a son, Lieut Col. John Paul (MacGregor) name assumed according to uncle's will. He was Deputy Auditor General of the Bengal Army. She married (2) 1786, John MacGregor (b 1765) Captain Royal Clan Alpine Fencibles, later Cashier Commercial Bank of Edinburgh. By this marriage she had, General Sir Duncan MacGregor K.C.B., Alexander, James, Mary, and Felicite.

18. Commissioned major in the army, August 19, 1819, and in the 31st Regiment, May 8, 1823. War Office, 5 February 1825, *A List of the Officers of the Army and Royal Marines on Full, Retired, and Half Pay with an Index*, 1825, p. 184, 31st (or Huntingdonshire) Regiment of Foot. *See also:* Edwin Hodder, *John MacGregor (Rob Roy)*, London: Hodder Brothers, 1894, p. 4; Alfred Edward John Cavendish, *An Reisimeid Chataich. The 93rd Sutherland Highlanders, now 2nd Bn. The Argyll and Sutherland Highlanders, Princess Louise's, 1799–1927*, London: Printed for private circulation, 1928, pp 74–75. Another account asserts that he had been first commissioned in the army in 1800 at the age of 13 following training at the Royal Military College, but the college Curator, Dr. Peter Thwaites, discounts the possibility, because the Junior Department was not founded until May 1802, and the course was usually at least a year, and more normally four or five years in length. Thwaites to Tracy, January 10 and 5, 2008.

19. *Times*, March 8, 1825; pg. 4; Issue 12595; col B, "Loss Of The Kent East Indiaman."

20. Robert Fearon, Ancestry.com. *Pallot's Marriage Index for England: 1780—1837, loc. cit.*; *Times*, Sep 17, 1821; pg. 3; Issue 11353; col F.

21. *Times*, March 13, 1830; pg. 4; Issue 14173; col F. SHC, ESR 2/15/2/2, Fearon family tree.

22. *Dumfrieshire Herald and Register*, March 19, 1858.

23. Hodder, pp. 3–6.

24. James Grant to Joseph Dart, 27 June 1825, BL/IOR, E/1/156 f. 755.

25. W. A. Shaw to Joseph Dart, 17 January 1825 (rec. 19 January), and Lushington, 27 December 1823, BL/IOR, E/1/156 f. 68.

26. Memorial at All Saints Royal Garrison Chuch, Aldershot.

27. SHC, ESR 2/15/2/2, Deputy Secretary at War to Messers Greenwood, Cox & Co., May 1825 (No 127960/112).

28. Hardy, pp. 72–73.

29. Sutton, p. 57.

30. Sutton, p. 103.

31. Hardy, pp. 91–92. That the following officer's births, fitted as above mentioned, and those only, be built upon the gun-deck, viz: One on the starboard

side, eight feet broad for the chief mate. One on the larboard side, seven feet six inches broad, for the second mate. Two on the starboard side, each seven feet broad, for third and fourth mates. Two on the larboard side, each seven feet broad, for the purser and surgeon. That a third mate's birth be on the starboard side, before the fourth mate's cabin, and a midshipman's birth on the larboard side, before the purser's cabin; and that two other cabins be before those already mentioned, each six feed six inches broad for the boatswain and carpenter. That the above cabins be built from the bulk-head of the great cabin, and on no account be carried further than the pumps. That the divisions between the cabins be made in such a manner, from the bulk-head of the great cabin, that each cabin may have a port. That no alteration be made to the above arrangements during the course of the voyage. That you do not, upon any consideration, partition off your great cabin, or make any division of the same, without the special orders of the Committee.

32. Hickey and Quennell, *A Prodigal Rake*, p. 104.

33. Edward William Bray to Loftus A. Bryan, 10 Bride Street, Dublin, Falmouth, March 10, 1825; transcript supplied by Daniel Feron, May 28, 2008.

34. BL/IOR, L/MAR/B34Q, February 19, 1825; Pearce, p. 152.

35. MacGregor, p. 6.

36. Thomas and William Daniell, *A Picturesque Voyage*.

37. BL/IOR, Eur MS G118, *Memoirs of William Hickey*, Hickey, v. I p. 133 and v. II p. 103.

38. Hardy, p. 97.

39. Charles Minchin and Sir Malcolm Alexander Morris, *Annals of an Anglo–Indian Family*, privately printed, ca. 1920.

40. Cotton, p. 41.

41. *Book of Common Prayer*, Oxford: Clarendon, 1815.

42. Sutton, p. 103.

43. Hardy, p. 98.

44. See: Robert Hamilton's *Mathematical Tables*, Edinburgh, 1790.

45. This was six meters west of the line presently shown at Greenwich, which is itself 102.5 meters west of that established by satellite, using an average of continental drifts.

46. Hardy, pp. 130–131.

47. BL/IOR, Eur MS G118, *Memoirs of William Hickey*, pp. 197–204; Hickey, v. II pp. 112–117.

CHAPTER 3: FATAL SPARK

1. Alfred Friendly, *Beaufort of the Admiralty: The Life of Sir Francis Beaufort, 1774–1857*, New York: Random House, 1977, pp. 142–147; Meteorological

Office, UK, "The Beaufort scale," http://www.metoffice .gov.uk/education/secondary/students/beaufort.html

2. James Capper, *Observations on the winds and monsoons : illustrated with a chart, and accompanied with notes, geographical and meteorological*, London (Printed by C. Whittingham...: and sold by J. Debrett ... [etc.], 1801.

3. Oil on canvas, support: 914 x 1219 mm., *Tate* N00530.

4. Ruskin, *Modern Painters*, American Publishers Corp.,5: 380–81.

5. MacGregor, p. 7.

6. Hodder, p. 10.

7. Townsend transcripts and *ESRJ* 2/33 p. 2.

8. Rimmell, p. 6. MacGregor says that "one of the officers of the ship" went down into the after hold to check on the cargo, and found that a barrel of spirits had come adrift. In the copy of the narrative believed to have belonged to Captain Spence of the 31st Regiment, the officer is identified as the third mate, Basil William Muir. IOR, MSS Eur A25, MacGregor, 1825 edition, Copy of Capt. Spence, 31st Regiment.

9. SHC: ESR/2/15/2/2, typescript entitled *The loss of the Kent: Statements of various NCOs etc*, 7 pp. Jack was discharged on March 24, 1828, "as being ineligible for further service in India. NA/PRO, WO 97/498.

10. Cannon, p. 87.

11. St. Luke 12 verses 4–8.

12. Townsend transcript, March 11, 1825, *ESRJ* 2/33 p. 2; Cannon, p. 89.

13. Edward William Bray to Loftus A. Bryan, 10 Bride Street, Dublin, Falmouth, March 10, 1825; transcript supplied by Daniel Feron, May 28, 2008.

14. Rimmell, p. 7.

15. MacGregor, p. 10.

16. MacGregor, p. 11.

17. Charles Dickens, *All Year Round*, November 24, 1866, p. 445.

18. MacGregor, p. 12.

19. MacGregor, p. 13.

20. Hodder, p. 11.

21. MacGregor, p. 13.

22. MacGregor, p. 15.

23. MacGregor, p. 16.

24. Townsend transcript, March 11, 1825, *ESJR* 2/33 p. 3.

25. MacGregor, p. 35.

CHAPTER 4: CAMBRIA

1. BL/IOR, L/MAR/B34Q.

2. Edward William Bray to Loftus A. Bryan, 10 Bride Street, Dublin,

Falmouth, March 10, 1825; transcript supplied by Daniel Feron, May 28, 2008.

3. NA/PRO BT 107/41 #22, *Cambria*. Hodder, p. 13.

4. NA/PRO BT 107/41 #22, *Cambria*.

5. Rimmell, p. 16.

6. Sharron P. Schwartz, "Creating the Cult of 'Cousin Jack:' Cornish Miners in Latin America 1812–1848 and the Development of an International Mining Labour Market," Institute of Cornish Studies December 1999, www.projects.ex.ac.uk/cornishlatin/Creating/20the/20Cult/20of/20Cousin/20Jack.pdf.

7. Letter from Valerie Hart, Assistant Librarian, Guildhall Library, July 16, 2007. From 1837 until 1840, the last London Trade Directory checked, the Mining Association was at 5 Broad Street Buildings, and from 1838 until at least 1840, the Anglo–Mexican Mint Company was at 9 New Broad Street.

8. According to a letter written to the *Times* by a proprietor of the Anglo–Mexican Association in September 1826, it worked in partnership with the Mexican owners of the mines. "The mine-owner says to the company, 'I have a mine which I prove to you by official records, [that] produced to me annually before the revolution, a large income, that now that the country is restored to peace and quietness, I have no capital with which to resume working my mine, and I can borrow none from my neighbours, for they are all in the same situation. Take the mine; therefore, under your management—restore it to a working condition; when it becomes productive [enough] to repay yourselves your outlay, and then for sixteen years, you shall have one-half the profits, and I will take the other; in the meantime you shall make me a stipulated alimentary allowance for my support, to be repaid, as well as your allowances, out of the first profits.'" *Times*, September 1, 1826, p. 3 issue 1306 col. B.

9. The Cornish in Latin America, http://www.projects.ex.ac.uk/cornishlatin/Lettercaptaingarby.htm

10. *Royal Cornwall Gazette*, Feb 19, 1825.

11. *Times*, November 24, 1824; pg. 2; Issue 12506; col A.

12. Communication from David Davies to Mike Gay, December 30, 2007. John Harland, *Seamanship in the Age of Sail*, Naval Institute Press, 1984, pp. 225–230.

13. Hodder, p. 12.

14. MacGregor, p. 7.

15. Rimmell, p. 10.

16. Townsend transcript, March 11, 1825, *ESRJ* 2/33 p. 3.

17. Hodder, pp. 12–13.

18. MacGregor, p. 19. See also Townsend, p. 10.

19. MacGregor, pp. 19–20.

20. Hodder, p. 13.

21. *Manual of Seamanship*, Vol. 2, London: HMSO, 1952, p. 270.

22. MacGregor, p. 20.

23. MacGregor, p. 21.

24. Communication from David Davis, December 31, 2007.

25. Rimmell, pp. 11–12.

26. BL/IOR, L/MAR/1—14 pp. 34–35.

27. *Manual of Seamanship*, Vol 1, 1908, By authority of the Lords Commissioners of the Admiralty, London, HMSO, 1908, pp. 194–196.

28. Hodder, p. 13.

29. *Times*, March 8, 1825, pg. 4; issue 12595; col. B, "Loss of the *Kent* East Indiaman." *See also: WBCA*, March 11, 1825.

30. Frederick Trestrail, *A Short Story of a Long Life*.

31. Townsend transcript, March 11, 1825, *ESRJ* 2/33 p. 3.

CHAPTER 5: COURAGE, FAITH, AND FIRE

1. Townsend transcript, March 11, 1825, *ESRJ* 2/33 p. 3.

2. MacGregor, p. 23.

3. Cannon, pp. 89–90.

4. Rimmell, pp. 12, 14; Townsend transcript, March 11, 1825, *ESRJ* 2/33 p. 3.

5. MacGregor, p. 9.

6. A report in the *West Briton and Cornwall Advertiser*, March 11, 1825, that the bowsprit was also used as a means of entering the boats is probably wrong, as neither MacGregor nor Townsend mention it, and as the fire was burning forward.

7. NMM, PAD6401 Kronheim, *Loss of the Kent East Indiaman*. Also: PAI9285. Kronheim had been born in Magdeburg, Germany, on October 26, 1810, moved to Edinburgh when he was 22, and finally established himself in London around 1846.

8. MacGregor, p. 30.

9. MacGregor, p. 34.

10. Townsend transcript, March 11, 1825, *ESRJ* 2/33 p. 3.

11. Hodder, p. 15.

12. MacGregor, p. 36.

13. MacGregor, p. 42.

14. Hodder, pp. 16–17.

15. MacGregor, p. 42.

16. Townsend transcript, March 11, 1825, *ESRJ* 2/33 p. 3.

CHAPTER 6: ABANDONED

1. MacGregor, p. 38.
2. NA/PRO, WO 43/233, William Cook to G. Smith, Falmouth, March 20, 1825.
3. MacGregor, p. 39.
4. MacGregor, pp. 42–43.
5. Hodder, p. 17.
6. Townsend transcript, March 11, 1825, *ESRJ* 2/33 p. 3; Rimmell, p. 15.
7. Cannon, p. 89.
8. MacGregor, Appendix 1, p. 60.
9. *Times*, March 17, 1825; pg 3; Issue 12603; Col. B, "The Kent East Indiaman."
10. Private George Burton did indeed die, but not a brother. NA/PRO WO 25/1698, Return of Dead, 31st Regiment, February 25 to March 25, 1825.
11. SHC: ESR/2/15/2/2.

CHAPTER 7: CAROLINE

1. MacGregor, Appendix 1, pp. 59–60. The appendix appears to have been taken from an anonymous source in the July 1825 edition of *The London Magazine*. "The details are exceedingly interesting," noted the magazine's editors, "and may be relied upon as authentic." *The London Magazine*, John Scott and John Taylor, eds., July 1825 (printed June), p. 335.
2. MUN, Maritime History Archives Dept., BT 107/129, p. 220, No. 26. Certificates of Registration, April 1, 1822, of Plantation build, and of re-registration, September 6, 1823.
3. Robert Bibby: NA/PRO, HO107; Piece 128; Book: 6; Civil Parish: Wallasey; County: Cheshire; Enumeration District: 8; Folio: 6; Page: 6; Line: 7; GSU roll: 241254; and HO107; Piece: 2174; Folio: 417; Page: 65; GSU roll: 87165-87167.
4. Ancestry.com. *Pallot's Marriage Index for England: 1780–1837*, database online, Provo, UT, USA: The Generations Network, Inc., 2001.
5. NA/PRO BT 98/83 # 147, *Caroline*.
6. *Lloyd's List* 1825, *Ships and Seafarers of Atlantic Canada*, St. John's, Nfld: Maritime History Archive, Memorial University of Newfoundland, c1998.
7. MacGregor, Appendix 1, p. 60.
8. MacGregor, Appendix 1, p. 61.
9. MacGregor, Appendix 1, p. 62.
10. MacGregor, Appendix 1, p. 64.
11. The last to give evidence was Private Thomas Wade, but Colonel Fearon was content with noting that he "gave nearly the same testimony as to the cir-

cumstances attending their escape and rescue as detailed by the preceding witnesses."

12. *Times*, March 11, 1825; pg. 3; Issue 12598; col C.

CHAPTER 8: LANDFALL

1. Hodder, p. 17.

2 . Townsend transcript, March 11, 1825, *ESRJ* 2/33, p. 3.

3. *Royal Cornwall Gazette*, March 5, 1825.

4. BL/IOR, L/MAR/B34Q, March 1.

5. MacGregor, Appendix. No. III., Cook to Messrs Wm. Broad and Sons,
Agents to Lloyd's., Ms Agents Brig *Cambria*, Falmouth, March 4, 1825;
BL/IOR, L/AG/1/6/27 p. 394.

6. NA/PRO, WO 43/233, Rescue of Crew and Passengers of Kent, William
Cook to G. Smith, Falmouth, March 20, 1825; and MacGregor, Appendix 3,
Cook to William Broad and Sons, Agents to Lloyd's, March 4, 1825.

7 . NA/PRO, WO25/1698, Return of 31st Regiment of Foot whose death
...etc., from February 25th to March 24, 1825, Drowned by the destruction of
the late ship *Kent*, March 1, 1825.

8. SHC, ESR 2/15/2/2, "Return of the 31st Regiment embarked on board the
Honorable Company's Ship *Kent* at Gravesend on the February 7, 1825."
Copy by C. Hordern.

9. Edward William Bray to Loftus A. Bryan, 10 Bride Street, Dublin,
Falmouth, March 10, 1825; transcript supplied by Daniel Feron, May 28,
2008.

10. Hodder, p. 18.

11. King had fought at the battle of Copenhagen in 1801 and as fourth lieutenant in Lord Nelson's flagship at the battle of Trafalgar in 1805. He died on
June 30, 1835, aged 61, in Falmouth. John Marshall, *Royal Naval Biography*,
vol 1 supplement part 1, p. 257; Robert Holden Mackenzie, *Trafalgar Roll*, p.
12.

12. *Times*, "Loss of the Kent East Indiaman," Falmouth, Saturday, March 5,
March 9, 1825, Issue 12596; col F. See also *The Annual Register*, 1825, p. 22.

13. *Royal Cornwall Gazette*, March 5, 1825.

14. MacGregor, p. 50.

15. Bray transcript, March 10, 1825.

16. No reference to this philanthropic work has been located in the minute
books of the Society of Friends in Cornwall, SF/24, 18, 19, 111, and 370.
Report by Sophie Trembath, Archive Assistant, Cornwall County Council,
305/07/11/16.

17. Frederick Trestrail, *The Short Story of a Long Life*.

18. Townsend transcript, March 11, 1825, *ESRJ* 2/33, p. 3.

19. Rimmell, p. 16.

20. *Voyage and Disaster—the Loss of the Kent*, http://www.queensroyalsur-reys.org.uk/reg_in_india/india04_1.html# 8 The Queen's Royal Surrey Regimental Association.

21. *WBCA*, April 8, 1825.

22. Townsend transcript, March 4, 1825.

23. Adrian Hopkins, "The Loss of the '*Kent*', East Indiaman," reproduced from the *Postal History Society Bulletin, East Surrey Regimental Journal*, November 1955, 7/4 pp. 19–20; and *The History of Wreck Covers*, p. 3. Unfortunately, Hopkins did not transcribe the letter itself.

24. Hedderwick, p. 45.

CHAPTER 9: HOME

1. Pearse, p. 135.

2. MacGregor, Appendix 4, p. 73.

3. *WBCA*, March 11, 1825; copied March 12 in the *Royal Cornwall Gazette*.

4. *WBCA*, March 25, 1825; MacGregor, Appendix 6, p. 76..

5. *Times*, March 11, 1825 pg. 3, Issue 12598, col C, and March 17, 1825; pg 3, Issue 12603, Col. B.

6. Lt-Col. R.B. Fearon, to the Adjutant-General, Horse-Guards, March 4, 1825, Cannon, pp. 86–87, and Pearce, p. 152.

7. Henry Torrens to Lt. Col. Fearon, March 7, 1825, Cannon, pp. 87–89. NA/PRO, WO 12/4668, Quarterly Pay List for 31st Regiment, December 25, 1824–March 24, 1825. BL/IOR, L/AG/1/6/27 p. 394.

8. MacGregor, Appendix. No. XIII, p. 88: Bryce Fearon, Lt. Col. 31st Foot. To the Chairman and Members of the Committee for the relief of the sufferers by the destruction of the Honourable Company's ship *Kent*, &c. Falmouth, March 16, 1825. *Times*, April 1, 1825; pg. 3; Issue 12616; col A.

9. SHC, ESR/2/15/2/2, copy of list referred to in the Deputy Secretary at War's letter of May 1825 (No 127900/112) to Messers Greenwood, Cox & Co.

10. BL/IOR, L/MIL/5/389 Coll 122 date: 1825—Copy correspondence on the claims of officers of HM 31st Foot who lost their baggage in the wreck of the *Kent*, ff 75–76. H. Taylor, Horse Guards, to George Harrison, Treasury, April 11.

11. Edward William Bray to Loftus A. Bryan, 10 Bride Street, Dublin, Falmouth, March 10, 1825; transcript supplied by Daniel Feron, May 28, 2008.

12. BL/IOR, L/MIL/5/389, ff. 75–79. Lt. General Sir H. Taylor, Horse Guards, to George Harrison, Treasury, 11 April, and see Feron to East India Co., 17 June 1828, forwarded by Taylor to J. Dart, Esq., Secretary to the Court of Directors, EIC, to Lt. General Sir H. Taylor.

13. BL/IOR, L/MIL/5/389, f. 81. J. Dart, Secretary to the Court of Directors, EIC, to Lt. General Sir H. Taylor.

14. SHC, ESR/2/15/2/2, (No 127900/112).

15. Pearse, p. 135.

16. SHC, ESR/2/15/2/2.

17. Cannon, p. 92.

18. *London Gazette*, April 2, 1825, no. 18123 p. 561.

19. BL/IOR, E/1/161, Joseph Dart to General Sir Herbert Taylor, 18, March 25, 1825.

20. Petition of Anne Currie, April 25, 1825; A Christie, Chatham, May 6, 1825, to Sir Herbert Taylor; Taylor to Joseph Dart, May 23, 1825: BL/IOR E/1/156 ff 552–556, Miscellaneous Letters Received; Cannon, p. 93. WO 12/4668, Quarterly Pay Lists for 31st Regiment, December 25, 1824—November 24, 1825.

21. NA/PRO, WO 97/500.

22. Pearse, p. 135; and Langley, pp. 37–43.

23. John Clark, *The History of India, from the Earliest Period to the Close of Lord Dalhousie's Administration*, London: Longmans, Green, Reader & Dyer, 1867.

24. Timothy Ash, "A Survivor—Private John Robinson—31st Foot: The Rescue by Captain Bibby, of the Brig *Caroline*, of 14 men of the 31st Foot from the East Indiaman *Kent* in 1825," *Journal of the Orders and Medals Research Society*, Autumn 1990, pp. 199–204.

25. For the previous voyage the purser had purchased £31/12/6 worth of goods which he subsequently sold for £439/1/6. BL/IOR L/MAR/B41R. See also *The Edinburgh Magazine and Literary Miscellany*, 1825, p. 503.

26. Charles Malcolm, *Regulations and Instructions for the Pursers of the Indian Navy*, Bombay, 1837, p. 35.

27. BL/IOR, L/MAR/1—13, pp. 778–80; Joseph Dart to John Carne, March 7, 1825; to Messers Dobson and Baker, March 7, 1825, E/1/161 (560, 559, 731).

28. Cotton p. 82; BL/IOR L/AG/1/6/27 p. 337 #61, 80.

29. MacGregor, Appendix. No. III., Cook to Messrs Wm. Broad and Sons, Agents to Lloyd's., Ms Agents Brig *Cambria*, Falmouth, March 4, 1825.

30. *WBCA* March 18, 1825 and MacGregor, Appendix 8–9, Duke of York to Captain Cook, Horse-Guards, March 9, 1825. Taylor's association with the Duke of York dated back to 1792. On June 13, 1805 he was appointed private secretary to King George III, a position he filled in a straightforward manner that earned him the good opinion of all, and in 1827 he was to be appointed secretary to the Duke of Wellington as Commander in Chief.

31. BL/IOR, Minutes of the Committee of Shipping, L/MAR/1-13, pp. 808–11; Joseph Dart to John Carne, 17, March 25, 1825; E/1/161.

32. BL/IOR, Minutes of the Committee of Shipping, L/MAR/1-13, pp. 808–11. J. Dart, East India House, to the Agents for the Ship *Cambria*, March 17, 1825, MacGregor Appendix 11.

33. BL/IOR, Minutes of the Committee of Shipping, L/MAR/1-15, December 13, 1826.

34. Royal Humane Society Annual Report , 1825, Appendix, pp. 48–50; 1826, pp. 36–47; Case Book entry 9862.

35. MacGregor Op. Cit., Appendix 12.

36. Communication by Huon Mallalieu, May 3, 2008.

37. Letter to the author from Daniel Fearon, June 2, 2008: "In those days I worked at Spink's the Coin delaers and a good client who was a dealer from Long Island appeared with a box of miniatures purchased at a house sale on the Island. He was on his way to Christie's, next door and when he showed them to me he said that he had been excited because of one being of Captain Cook, but it wasn't the 'right' Captain Cook. I was able to say that he had picked about the only person in the world to whom this was indeed the 'right' one, and so it was purchased. My uncle died a quite a while ago, '84 I think, then when my Aunt died my sister [Mary Wallace] ended up with the *Kent* pictures." See also, SHC, ESR/1/12/7; list of items of note from the Royal United Services Museum; ESR/2/15/2/2, Correspondence between Charles Horden and Captain R.J. Berrow, East Surrey Regiment, September 8, 1959.

38. BL/IOR, L/MAR/1-13, pp. 819–20.

39. BL/IOR, L/MAR/1-13, pp. 834–35.

40. BL/IOR, E/1/156 ff. 250–51, James Milligan to Joseph Dart, Liverpool, March 19, 1825.

41. BL/IOR, L/MAR/1-14, pp. 34–35, Minutes of the Committee of Shipping; E/1/161 (745) Joseph Dart to James Milligan, March 26, 1825.

42. BL/IOR, L/MAR/1-14, pp. 34–35, 94. Minutes of the Committee of Shipping, April 27, and 18 May 1825.

43. BL/IOR, L/MAR/1-14, pp. 34–35, Minutes of the Committee of Shipping, April 27, 1825,

44. BL/IOR, L/MAR/1-13 p. 842, Minutes of the Committee of Shipping.

45. *Times*, April 13, 1825; pg. 2; Issue 12626; col A.

46. BL/IOR, Minutes of the Committee of Shipping, L/MAR/1-16, February 14, 1827.

47. *Times,* November 1, 1862; pg. 5; Issue 24392; col F.

48. Farrington, *A Biographical Index*.

49. http://bmagic.org.uk/people/+Thomas+Halliday.

50. NMM, MEC2131 and MEC2130, medal commemorating the loss of the East Indiaman *Kent*, 1825, Thomas Halliday, 1825. Daniel Fearon, "The Melancholy loss of the *Kent*, East Indiaman—1825: An Account of the Medal

Struck to Commemorate the Event," *The Orders and Medals Research Society*, Winter 1988, pp. 244–252. BL/IOR, Minutes of the Committee of Shipping, L/MAR/1-15, September 26, 1826. Examples of the named medals are: John MacKenney (Col. F. R. T. T. Gascoigne Collection); William Cook (Mary Wallace); Mr. Joseph Hemsley (Christie's April 30, 1991, lot 273, part); David Ritchie (Sotheby's November 16, 2001, lot 450); Joseph Pascoe, John Platts (Bonhams July 14, 2004, lot 76); Mr. William Parker (*Spink Numismatic Circular*, medal supplement, January 1988).

51. Ancestry.com. *Pallot's Marriage Index for England*: 1780–1837.

52. NA/PRO, Registrar General of Shipping, Port of London, BT 107/41 # 22, *Cambria*.

53. MUN, Maritime History Archives Dept., BT 107/131 p. 278 No. 80.

54. MUN, Maritime History Archives Dept., BT 107/493 p. 270 No. 5.

55. BL/IOR, L/AG/1/6/27 p. 394 (#640); NA/PRO, BT 98/83 #147, Board of Trade, Muster Role for the *Caroline*.

56. *Times*, April 28, 1830; pg. 4; Issue 14212; col A; July 19, 1830; pg. 3, Issue 14282, col B; December 6, 1832, pg. 4, Issue 15028; col D; December 31, 1832, pg. 4, Issue 15049, col D; October 03, 1835; pg. 1; Issue 15911; col C.

57. Communication, January 5, 2008 14:17:09 -0000 from Sandy Williamson, Enterprise, Trade & Investment, Belfast.

58. NA/PRO, HO107; Piece 128; Book: 6; Civil Parish: Wallasey; County: Cheshire; Enumeration District: 8; Folio: 6; Page 6; Line: 7; GSU roll: 241254; and HO107; Piece: 2174; Folio: 417; Page: 65; GSU roll: 87165-87167, Robert Bibby:

59. According to the registry of Deaths, a two Robert Bibbys died at Wigan in 1856, and another at Warrington.

60. NA/PRO WO 43/233 ff. 159–172, Minutes of Anglo–Mexican Association, March 8, 1825; Covering letter by Joseph Lowe to Secretary at War; W. Morton Dhy, Navy Office, to William Merry, March 25, 1824.

61. *Times*, December 3, 1825; pg. 2; Issue 12827; col A.

62. *Times*, August 25, 1826; pg. 2; Issue 13055; col F, "The Money-Market."

63. *Times*, September 6, 1826; pg. 3; Issue 13065; col B, and January 4, 1827; pg. 3; Issue 13167; col B.

64. *Times*, October 16, 1826, Issue 13092, Col F.

65. *Times*, April 22, 1834; pg. 5; Issue 15458; col C; and May 13, 1834; pg. 2; Issue 15476; col E.

66. *Times*, November 12, 1845; pg. 8; Issue 19079; col F, "The Mint of Guanaxuato and the Mexican Government."

67. *Times*, November 1, 1842; pg. 5; Issue 18129; col A, "Money-Market and City Intelligence."

68. *Times*, April 3, 1848; pg. 7; Issue 19827; col A, "Money-Market And City Intelligence."

69. *Times*, December 6, 1853; pg. 5; Issue 21604; col A, "Money-Market And City Intelligence."

70. *Times*, April 5, 1853, pg. 6; Issue 21394; col. F: letter to the editor from C. Richardson, 15 Charles-Street, St. James's, April 4.

71. *Times*, April 26, 1858; pg. 6; Issue 22977; col B, and April 18, 1859; pg. 7; Issue 23283; col A, "Money-Market and City Intelligence."

72. *Narrative of the Loss of the Kent East Indiaman, by fire, in the Bay of Biscay, on March 1, 1825, in a Letter to a Friend by a Passenger*. First published anonymously in Edinburgh in 1825, by Waugh & Innes, the *Narrative* was reprinted in Edinburgh in 1826, and then in 1830 it appeared in Dublin published by P.D Hardy for the Society for Promoting the United and Scriptural Education, when it was properly attributed to MacGregor. An edition appeared in Glasgow that same year, and an abridgment was published in 1834 in London under the imprint of J.G. and F. Rivington. MacGregor's full text was first published in London in 1834 by the Society for Promoting Christian Knowledge; reprinted in 1842; and in 1859 it was taken up by the Religious Tract Society. In 1861 an Italian translation was published in Torino.

73. MacGregor, p. 35; and Hodder, p. 21.

74. Hodder, pp. 21–30.

75. Cavendish, *An Reisimeid Chataich*, p. 64.

76. *Times*, March 19, 1836; pg. 5; Issue 16055; col B.

77. Hodder, p. 30. Cavendish, p 77, referring to the *Toronto Colonist*, April 1839.

78. Cavendish, p. 74. Refers to Captain I. H. Mackay Scobie: *An Old Highland Fencible Corps: the history of the Reay Fencible Highland Regiment of Foot, or Mackay's Highlanders, 1794–1802, with an account of its services in Ireland during the Rebellion of 1798*. W. Blackwood & Sons: Edinburgh & London, 1914.

79. Police Services of Northern Ireland, Inspectors-General and Chief Constables from 1836; *The Edinburgh Gazette*, October 26, 1858, No. 1854.

80. Hodder, p. 50.

81. *Hart's army list, and militia list*. London, J. Murray, n. 75 1857, p. 4.; *The Edinburgh Gazette*, November 14, 1851, No. 6125 (Knighted December 26, 1848).

82. *Times*, August 5, 1854; pg. 8; Issue 21812; col A.

83. *Freeman's Journal*, Sept. 28, 1877; *Dumfrieshire Herald and Register*, 19.3.1858; *Edinburgh Gazette*, December 22, 1857, No. 1302.

84. NA/PRO, RG9; Piece: 9; Folio: 5; Page: 7; GSU roll: 542555.

85. *Edinburgh Gazette*, November 14, 1864, No. 1427; *London Gazette*, October 2, 1877, No. 24508.

86. NA/PRO, RG11; Piece: 726; Folio: 29; Page: 4; GSU roll: 1341169.

87. SHC, ESR 2/13/2 p. 8 #6. *England and Wales, BMD Death Index: 1881,* General MacGregor's death was registered in Greenwich, second quarter 1881, vol. 1, p. 568. MacGregor's orders and medals were sold at Christies to Matthew Taylor, a Glasgow collector, on November 23, 1990, Lot 525, for £3,600.

88. Hodder, p. 21.

89. *Times,* May 24, 1825; pg. 3; Issue 12661; col A.

90. SHC, ESR 2/15/2/2, Copies by C. Hordern of correspondence and notes relating to the Freedom of Cork.

91. *London Gazette,* January 28, 1826, no. 18215 p. 177; and June 3, 1828 no. 18457 p. 1073; *Times,* December 15 1829, pg. 4; Issue 14097; col. C.

92. *Times,* March 13, 1830; pg. 4; Issue 14173; col F.

93. Daniel Fearon, "The Melancholy loss of the *Kent,* East Indiaman–1825; an Account of the Medal Struck to Commemorate the Event," *The Orders and Medals Research Society,* Winter 1988, p. 244.

94. *Times,* November 24, 1838, and February 14, 1839, Issues 16895 p. 3 Col. F, and 16965 p. 5 Col. C.

95. BL/IOR Eur Mss F100, Fearon (Robert Bryce), Maj-Gen. *Annual Register* 1851, p. 256, date January 26; NA/PRO Registry of Births, Deaths, and Marriage, Bishops Stortford, March 1851, Bishop's Stortford, 6, 367. A death notice in the *Times* for another officer (Friday, August 31, 1849, p. 7, issue 20269, col. B) erroneously gives Fearon's death in 1844, but it got it more or less right on February 5, 1851, p. 7, issue 20717, col. F. Colburn's *United Service Magazine* gave his death date as January 20. A Margaret Eliza Palmer died in Sudbury the first quarter of 1867, age 60: Death Index, Sudbury District, vol. 4a.

96. Townsend, March 11, 1825, *ESRJ* 2/33 p. 4.

97. Rimmell narrative.

98. Trestrail, The Short Story of a Long Life. Reverend Trestrail (1803–90) acted as home Secretary of te Baptist Missionary Society from 1849–70.

99. BL/IOR, Minutes of the Committee of Shipping, L/MAR/1-15, April 12, 1826.

100. *Times,* July 9, 1857; pg. 11; Issue 22728; col E.

101. *Times,* May 13, 1858; pg. 10; Issue 22992; col B.

102. BL/IOR Eur MS A59, Obituary inside cover dated January 6, 1878.

103. BL/IOR Eur MS A59.

104. Arbuthnot, Sir Alexander John (1822–1907), by F. H. Brown, (reviewed by Robert Eric Frykenberg). *Dictionary of National Biography,* article/30430.

105. Sutton, p. 126.

106. BL/IOR Eur MS A59, Obituary inside cover, n.d.

CHAPTER 10: A STORY FOR THE AGES

1. Hoare, Edward Newenham, Vicar of Stoneycroft, *Perils of the Deep, being an account of some of the remarkable shipwrecks and disasters at sea during the last hundred years. . . With map.*, London: Christian Knowledge Society, 1885, pp. 138–147. Lucy Delap, "Thus does man prove his fitness to be the master of things": *Shipwrecks and Chivalry in Edwardian Britain*, http://www.corpus.cam.ac.uk/crosstalk/delap.html.
2. Hoare, pp. 38–39.
3. Charles Dickens, *All Year Round*, November 24, 1866, p. 444.
4. MacGregor, pp. 53–54.
5. Donald A. Rosenthal, "Gericault's 'Raft of the Medusa' and Caravaggio," *The Burlington Magazine*, Vol. 120, No. 909 (Dec., 1978), pp. 836–841.

Bibliography

ARCHIVES

British Library, India Office Records European Manuscripts

A59, Annotations by Henry Elmsley Busteed (1833–1912), Madras Medical Service 1855–86, *A Narrative of the Loss of the Kent East Indiaman*, (3rd edn Edinburgh 1825).

G118, William Hickey Memoirs.

J627, James Spence, Copy of 1st edition of *A Narrative of the Loss of the Kent East Indiaman* (Edinburgh 1825) marginally annotated by Capt. James Spence, British Army, one of the passengers, with the names of persons referred to anonymously in the narrative. See printed catalogue for full description; requisition as Mss Eur A 25.

B/177–178, Minutes of the Court of Directors, 1825.

E/1/156, Miscellaneous Letters Received.

L/AG/1/6/27, Accountant General Department, General Commercial Journal.

L/AG/1/7/1, Journal of Private Trade, 1 May 1821.

L/MAR/1/13–15, Minutes of the Committee of Shipping, April 1824–April 1827.

L/MAR/B/34Q, Log of *Scaleby Castle*, 20 December 1824–16 June 1826

L/MAR/B 41 I, *Kent* Journal to 29 March 1824, 2 Voyage.

L/MAR/B/41Q(1–2), Ledger, *Kent*, c.1821–c.1822.

L/MAR/B41R(1–2), Ledger of Wages, *Kent*, Second Voyage, 1824.

L/MAR/B/41S, Imprest Book of *Kent* 1824/5.

L/MIL/5/389, Military Department Special Collections: Collection 122, 1786–1845.

Memorial University of Newfoundland, Maritime History Archives Department

BT 107/129, p. 220, No. 26. Certificates of Registration, 1 April 1822, of Plantation build, and of re-registration, 6 September 1823.

National Archives, Public Records Office

ADM 35/316: 3, Admiralty, *Caroline*'s Pay Book.

ADM 51/1261 and 1381, Admiralty, Captain's Logs.

ADM 102/706 and 707, Admiralty, Port Mahon Hospital Records.

BT 98/83, Board of Trade, Registry of Shipping and Seamen: Agreements and Crew Lists, Series I, Liverpool, 1824–1825, #147, *Caroline*.

BT 107/34, Board of Trade, # 25, Registration of London Foreign Trade, *Kent*.

BT 107/41, Board of Trade, Registration of London Foreign Trade, *Cambria*.

BT 111/4, Board of Trade, Registry of Shipping and Seamen: Transcripts and Transactions, Indexes to Transcripts, Ships Names: A—Z, London, 1824—1832.

CUST 130/3, Customs and Excise and predecessors: Registry of British Ships: London Port: Title Registers, 1819–1821, # 287, *Kent*.

HO107, Census 1841–1851, Piece 128; Book: 6; Civil Parish: Wallasey; County: Cheshire; Enumeration District: 8; Folio: 6; Page: 6; Line: 7; GSU roll: 241254.

HO107; Census 1841–1851, Piece: 2174; Folio: 417; Page: 65; GSU roll: 87165-87167.

PRO 30/2/7/9, India. Chairman and Deputy Chairman of the East India Company. List, India. Directors of the East India Company. List, 1773–1853.

WO 43/233, War Office, Rescue of crew and passengers (of 31st Regiment) of wrecked East Indiaman *Kent* by Anglo–Mexican Association's ship *Cambria*, 1825.

WO 12/4668, War Office, 31st of Foot, Quarterly Pay List, 25 December 1824–24 November 1825.

WO 25/1698, 31 Foot. 1 Battalion. Casualty returns 1824–1828.

WO 97/498, 500. Discharge Papers.

Surrey History Centre

ESR 1/12/3, Scrapbook.

ESR 1/12/7, Scrapbook.

ESR 2/13/2, Scrapbook.

ESR 2/13/24, Album.

ESR 2/15/2/2, Records of the Royals and East Surrey Regiment.

ESR 2/15/2/8, Photocopy of *Orders and Medal Research Society Journal*.

PRIVATE COLLECTIONS

Transcript of letter from Edward William Bray to Loftus A. Bryan, 10 Bride Street, Dublin, Falmouth, March 10, 1825, supplied by Daniel Fearon, May 28, 2008.

Transcripts of letters from Dr. Edward Richard Townsend made by C. E. C. Townsend, March 1988.
Note: Both transcripts are of documents once found at the Falmouth Public Library, but now missing.

Periodicals and Journals

The Annual Register, 1851.
The Christian Journal and Literary Register, 1827.
Colburn's United Service Magazine
Dumfrieshire Herald and Register.
The Edinburgh Gazette.
The Edinburgh Magazine and Literary Miscellany, 1825.
Hart's army list, and militia list. London, J. Murray, n. 75 1857.
Journal of the Orders and Medals Research Society
Kent's Original London Directory, London, 1816 and 1825 editions.
The Knickerbocker, or New-York Monthly Magazine, 1834.
London Gazette.
The London Magazine.
The Naval Chronicle, London, 1797–1818.
Royal Cornwall Gazette.
Royal Military Calendar
The Times Digital Archive, 1765–1985.

Books and Articles

Admiralty, *Manual of Seamanship*, Vol 1, London, HMSO, 1908.
Admiralty, *Manual of Seamanship*, Vol. 2, London: HMSO, 1952.
Anon. *Dangers of the deep; or, Narratives of shipwreck and adventure at sea*, 1854
Ash, Timothy, "A Survivor—Private John Robinson—31st Foot: The Rescue by Captain Bibby, of the Brig *Caroline*, of 14 Men of the 31st Foot from the East Indiaman *Kent* in 1825," *Journal of the Orders and Medals Research Society*, Autumn 1990, pp. 199–204.
Boase, George Clement and William Prideaux Courtney, *Bibliotheca Cornubiensis. A catalogue of the writings. . . of Cornishmen, and of works relating to the county of Cornwall, etc.* 3 vol., London: Longmans & Co., 1874–82.
Bouguer, Pierre, *Traite du Navire, de sa Construction, et de ses Mouvemens*, 1746.
Brown, Ruth Rhynas, "Guns carried on East Indiamen, 1600–1800," *International Journal of Nautical Archaeology*, February 1990, Vol. 19 Issue 1, pp. 17–22.

Cavendish, Alfred Edward John, *An Reisimeid Chataich. The 93rd Sutherland Highlanders, now 2nd Bn. The Argyll and Sutherland Highlanders, Princess Louise's, 1799–1927*, London: Printed for private circulation, 1928.

Capper, James, *Observations on the winds and monsoons : illustrated with a chart, and accompanied with notes, geographical and meteorological*, London (Printed by C. Whittingham ... : and sold by J. Debrett ... [etc.], 1801.

Chatterton, E. Keble, *The Old East Indiamen*, Philidelphia, J.B. Lippincott Co., [1914].

John Clark, *The History of India, from the Earliest Period to the Close of Lord Dalhousie's Administration*, London: Longmans, Green, Reader & Dyer, 1867.

Daniell, Thomas and William, *A Picturesque Voyage to India by way of China*, London, 1816.

Darwin, Charles, and Frederick Burkhardt, Sydney Smith, David Kohn, William Montogmery, eds., *The Correspondence of Charles Darwin*, vols 1–3, Cambridge: Cambridge University Press, 1985.

Delap, Lucy, "Thus does man prove his fitness to be the master of things": *Shipwrecks and Chivalry in Edwardian Britain*, http://www.corpus.cam .ac.uk/crosstalk/delap.html.

Dickens, Charles, *All Year Round*, November 24, 1866, p. 444.

Farrington, Anthony, *A Biographical Index of East India Company Maritime Service Officers, 1600–1834*, British Library, 1999.

————, *Catalogue of East India Company Ship's Journals and Logs, 1600–1834*, London: British Library, 1999.

Fearon, Daniel, "The Melancholy loss of the Kent, East Indiaman–1825; an Account of the Medal Struck to Commemorate the Event," *The Orders and Medals Research Society*, Winter 1988, p. 244.

Fearon, S. P., *Pedigrees of the Fearon Family Trading into China and Notes on Collateral and Other Matters of Family Interest*, private printing, n.d.

Friendly, Alfred, *Beaufort of the Admiralty: The Life of Sir Francis Beaufort, 1774–1857*, New York: Random House, 1977.

Hackman, Rowan, *Ships of the East India Company*, Gravesend: World Ship Society, 2001.

Hardy, Charles, and Horatio Charles A. Hardy, *Registry of Ships*, 4 ed., London, 1835.

Harland, John, *Seamanship in the Age of Sail*, Naval Institute Press, 1984.

Harris, R. H., Commander R.N., *Captain Alston's Seamanship*, New Edition, Portsmouth: Griffin & Co., 1871.

Hedderwick, James, *The English Orator, A Selection of Pieces for Reading and Recitation*, Glasgow, 1833.

Hickey, William, and Alfred Spencer, ed., *Memoirs of William Hickey, 1749–1809*, 4 vols., London: Hurst & Blackett, 1913.

Hickey, William, and Peter Quennell, ed., *The Prodigal Rake: Memoirs of William Hickey*, New York: E. P{. Dutton & Co., 1962.

Hodder, Edwin, *John MacGregor (Rob Roy)*, London: Hodder Brothers, 1894.

Hopkins, Adrian, "The Loss of the 'Kent', East Indiaman," reproduced from the Postal History Society Bulletin, *East Surrey Regimental Journal*, November 1955.

Langley, Michael J., *The East Surrey Regiment, (The 31st and 70th Regiments of Foot)*, London: Leo Cooper, 1972.

Leslie, Charles Robert, *Memoirs of the Life of John Constable*, 1843. Reprint, London: John Lehmann, 1949.

MacGregor, Duncan, *A Narrative of the loss of the Kent East Indiaman, by fire, in the Bay of Biscay, on the 1st March, 1825, in a letter to a friend [signed, Servatus]. By a Passenger* [i.e. Sir D. Macgregor], Edinburgh, 1825. Also reprinted under the title, *The Loss of the Kent East Indiaman in the Bay of Biscay. Narrated in a Letter to a Friend.*

Mackenzie, Robert Holden, *The Trafalgar roll: the ships and the officers*; introduction by Colin White, London: Chatham, 2004.

Malcolm, Charles, *Regulations and Instructions for the Pursers of the Indian Navy*, Bombay, 1837

Marshall, John, *Royal Naval Biography, or, Memoirs of the services of all the Flag Officers, Superannuated Rear-Admirals, Retired-Captains, Post-Captains, and Commanders. . . on the Admiralty list. . . Illustrated by a series of historical and explanatory notes, etc.*, London, 1823–1835.

Memorial University of Newfoundland, *Lloyd's List 1825, Ships and Seafarers of Atlantic Canada*, St. John's, Nfld: Maritime History Archive, 1998.

Minchin, Charles, and Sir Malcolm Alexander Morris, *Annals of an Anglo–Indian Family*, privately printed, ca. 1920.

Pearse, Hugh W., *History of the 31st Foot Huntingdonshire Regt. 70th Foot Surrey Regt. subsequently 1st & 2nd Battalion*, 1916.

[Rimmell, Reverend Edgcombe], *A Narrative of the Loss by Fire of the Honourable East [India] Company's Ship Kent on Her Voyage to India*, Falmouth: Printed by and for J. Philip, Bookseller, and sold by J. Richardson, Royal Eschange, London, [March 16, 1825].

Robertson, James Peter. *Personal Adventures and Anecdotes of an Old Officer*, London: Edward Arnold, 1906.

Rogers, Thomas J. H., Master of the Band, *Grand Quick March of the 31st Regiment*, London, Mess. R. Cocks & Co., n.d.

Rosenthal, Donald A., "Gericault's 'Raft of the Medusa' and Caravaggio," *The Burlington Magazine*, Vol. 120, No. 909 (Dec., 1978), pp. 836–841.

Ruskin, John, *Modern Painters*, American Publishers Corp., n.d.

Schwartz, Sharron P., "Creating the Cult of 'Cousin Jack:' Cornish Miners in Latin America 1812–1848 and the Development of an International Mining Labour Market," Institute of Cornish Studies December 1999, www.projects.ex.ac.uk/cornishlatin/Creating%20the%20Cult%20of%20Cousin%20Jack.pdf.

Shaw, Frank Hubert, *Full Fathom Five: A Book of Famous Shipwrecks*, New York: The Macmillan Company, 1930.

Shellin, Maurice, *India and the Daniells*, London: Inchcape, 1979.

Speedy, Allan, Ed., *Mrs Livingstone I presume, Memoirs of Sarah Speedy, Waterloo to Waikato*, http://www.speedy.co.nz/recollections/

Sutton, Jean, Lords of the East, the East India Company and its Ships, London: Conway Maritime Press, 1981.

Townsend, Dr. Edward, "Dr. Edward Richard Townsend's letter," *East Surrey Regiment Journal*, August 1927, Vol. 2 no. 33 p 2.

Tracy, Nicholas, *Naval Chronicle, Consolidated Edition*, London: Chatham Publication, 1999.

Trestail, Reverend Frederick with Elizabeth Ryland Trestrail, ed., *The Short Story of a Long Life. Memorials of F. Trestrail. . . . Edited by his Widow,* London: Alexander & Shepheard, [1894].

War Office, 5 February 1825, *A List of the Officers of the Army and Royal Marines on Full, Retired, and Half Pay with an Index*, 1825.

Warneford, Lieutenant Robert, R.N., pseud. [William Russell], *The Jolly Boat; or, Perils and Disasters Illustrating Courage, Endurance, and Heroism in the Merchant-Marine Service*, London: John Maxwell and Co., 1865.

Index

seasickness, 68, 70, 72
Sexton, James, 15, 16, 31, 64, 180
ship's stores, 28, 32, 149
signal of distress, 82
Sikh war, 170
smoke, 63, 69, 70, 71, 72, 82, 86, 115, 139, 144, 154
Society of Friends, 156, 158
soldiers, 4, 6, 9, 10, 18, 36, 42, 44, 51, 54, 65, 68, 69, 70, 72, 73, 75, 87, 90, 100, 102, 105, 106–108, 112–114, 116–120, 126, 128, 129, 134, 151, 154–156, 158, 163, 166, 168, 169, 171, 173, 177, 190, 201, 202, 203
spanker boom, 4, 109–112, 116, 118, 119, 128, 131, 133, 134, 143
Spence, James, 45, 69, 70, 73, 100
spirits, alcoholic, 29, 31, 50, 66, 67, 78, 114, 122, 177, 178
St. Helena, 16, 19
St. Ives, Cornwall, 159, 182
stoicism, 75
stowage, 31, 64
survivors, 1, 3, 4, 5, 85, 86, 96, 99, 129, 130, 131, 132, 144–146, 149–152, 154, 155, 159, 165, 166, 172, 177, 196, 200, 204

Thames, river, 13, 29, 35, 37, 40, 43, 44, 49, 85, 88, 91, 177
13th Light Infantry, 12
31st Regiment, 3, 9, 32, 38–42, 45, 46, 59, 112, 114, 130, 154, 163, 165, 169, 181, 203
Thomson, John, 16, 81, 92, 96–98, 100, 102, 103, 105, 126, 128, 181
threat of fire, 56

Tighe, Mr., 16, 176
Titanic, 6
total complement, 23
Townsend, Edward Richard, 3, 4, 44, 66, 69, 77, 90, 93, 103, 106, 108, 118, 123, 128, 151, 152, 157, 159, 194–196
Trafalgar, battle of, 38, 210, 219
Truro, Cornwall, 159, 182
Turner, Joseph M. W., 62, 63, 65

uniforms, East India Company, 19; 31st Regiment, 39, 167

Vera Cruz, Mexico, 83, 173
Victory, 37, 38

wages, 24, 46, 166, 201
Wales, 82, 83, 225
Wallen, Matthew, 141–146, 175, 177
warehouses, 24, 28
Warren, James, 10, 100, 178
waterline, 26, 40, 96
wives, 40, 42, 46, 52, 70, 73, 90, 100, 106, 119, 154, 155, 168
women, 40, 42, 45, 54, 68, 70, 72, 105, 106, 117, 119, 154, 193, 196, 203
women and children, precedence in rescue, 87, 90, 95, 97, 100, 107, 108, 112, 121, 151, 155, 158, 164, 197, 199, 204

Yorkshire smelterers, 9, 83, 98

Acknowledgments

THE author owes a great deal to the assistance of Mike Gay, who was invaluable in searching the internet and provided a sounding board for ideas, and to Daniel Fearon and his sister Mary Wallace who provided otherwise inaccessible transcripts of original material and other documentation and pictures relative to the story of the *Kent*. The author is also deeply grateful for the assistance of many archivists and librarians: Rod Mackenzie, Archivist/Assistant Curator, Argyle and Sutherland Museum; Andrea Wellstead, PA/Administrator, Christ's Hospital; Penny Brooke, Head, and Margaret Makepeace, India Office Records, British Library; David Thomas, Archivist and Sophie Trembath Assistant Archivist, Cornwall Records Office; Vanessa Bourguignon, Library Officer, Cornish Studies Library; Sandy Williamson, Department of Enterprise, Trade & Investment; Charlie Turpie, Principal Archivist and Valerie Hart, Assistant Librarian, Guildhall Library; Paula Marshall, Senior Clerk, Maritime History Archive, Memorial University of Newfoundland; Alastair Massie, Robert Fleming, and Justin Saddington, National Army Museum; David Taylor, Picture Librarian, and Andrew Mitchell and Andrew Choong, Curators, Historic Photographs & Ship Plans Section, National Maritime Museum; Susanne Kittlinger, Image Sales Executive, Science &

Society Picture Library, Science Museum; Duncan Sutton, Team Leader, and Guzman Gonzalez, Surrey History Centre; Dr. Peter Thwaites, Curator of the Sandhurst Collection, Royal Military College; Ian EJ Chatfield, Curator, the Queen's Royal Surrey Regiment Museum; William W. Lowe and Joseph T. Vallejo, Vallejo Gallery; private scholars, Andrea Cordani of "East India Company Ships;" David Davies, Merchant Mariner; John Harland, scholar of square rig shipping; my student Kristin McLellan; and most particularly, at the University of New Brunswick Library, Joanna Smyth, Reference Librarian, and the staff of the document delivery section.